At Your Fingertips

"Answering Who, What, When, How and Why the Rosary"

By Stacy Mal

At Your Fingertips, December 2017

Published by Stacy Mal   Pennsylvania, USA

www.StacyMal.com

ISBN 9781973550150

To the Blessed Virgin Mary, with all my heart.

INTRODUCTION

What

What if I told you there was a prayer you could pray that could transform your life and save the world? What if I told you it has already saved countless lives, converted the most hardened sinners, cured people of fatal disease, caused the devil to flee, and won seemingly impossible wars? What if Jesus Himself asked us to pray it? What if the justice of God could be appeased by it?

Would you pray it? Most, I presume, would answer yes.

But, what if I told you this "miracle prayer" is the Rosary? The answer, then, might be quite different for some. Most of my Protestant friends would likely say no, they would not pray it. Even many of my Catholic friends would decline—because even though the Rosary is one of the most powerful prayers there is, it is also one of the most misunderstood. Many *mistakenly* assume the Rosary to be either idolatrous or blasphemous or fanatical.

But what if I told you the Rosary was none of these things? What if I told you this prayer gives more glory to God and calls down more grace for souls than anything else we could utter? What if I told you the Rosary has been misunderstood because the devil himself has attacked it? What if I told you he fears this prayer more than any other devotion? What if I told you it is the weapon of His undoing, and the sole weapon that can obtain peace for the world?

Would I pique your curiosity enough that you would listen to more information?

In this book, I would like to tell you about all of this. I would like to explain this mysterious prayer called the Rosary, which has been so dreadfully misinterpreted over the years. And I am begging you—no matter who you are: Catholic, protestant, atheist, whoever—to open your heart to what I have to say.

Please, friend. Please, don't discount this book because of something you were told by a friend or pastor who did not understand it. Don't discount this book on account of a preconceived notion you made before you had all the facts. Seek to understand the Rosary first, with knowledge regarding its background and purpose, and then formulate your opinion and make your decision.

If what I say is true—if the Rosary is the weapon that is to unite the army of God, defeat the devil, and save the world—then don't you owe it to the Lord to at least open yourself to the possibility? Also, there is no harm in _seeking_ truth. There is only harm in accepting untruth.

"Ask, and it will be given to you; seek, and you will find; knock, and it will be opened to you." (Matthew 7:7) By reading this book you are not accepting anything yet. You are merely seeking truth... a noble and Godly thing.

Why

Why have I chosen to write this book? Well, for several reasons. The first reason is because the Rosary has transformed my life and it saddens me deeply that it's so misunderstood. The second reason is because the Lord God put it on my heart to do so...and when the Lord puts something on your heart, He does so with fire. He fans flames within a soul that burn so intensely you cannot extinguish them. You can only quench them with obedience. So here I am, quenching the thirst of the Lord, which has manifested as fire in my heart. So, forgive me if, at points in this book, I seem overzealous. It is the only way I know how to project my heart onto the page.

That being said, if a small flame from any of these pages somehow sparks your own heart (even in the slightest way), know that it is the Lord Himself moving in you. Do not run from it. Do not squelch it with doubt. Do not let mortal thoughts trample the new flickering of Divine Light. Let the breath of the Holy Spirit breathe upon it until it increases and burns as our Lord desires it should.

When

When did I decide to move forward with this book? I made the pledge to Jesus and Mary on the feast of Our Lady of the Rosary, while on a pilgrimage praying the Rosary with thousands of others. I was moved interiorly to do it with a deep, profound knowledge that NOW IS THE TIME.

Unfortunately, I came home from that pilgrimage and got sucked back into daily life. My new resolve to write about the Rosary fell to the wayside while other things took priority over it. That is, until one morning when I was reading a book by St. Louis de Montfort.

St. Louis told the story of Blessed Alan de la Roche—a Dominican Father from a monastery in Brittany. He was a distinguished theologian, famous for his sermons. One day, Jesus appeared to Blessed Alan and said to him, "You are crucifying me...because you have all the learning and understanding that you need to preach my Mother's Rosary, and you are not doing it. If you only did that, you could teach many souls the right path and lead them away from sin. But you are not doing it, and so you yourself are guilty of the sins they commit."

When I read those words, it was as if Jesus spoke them directly to my heart. It was as if I heard them, not read them. I am not a theologian like Blessed Alan, but for some reason the Lord put this understanding of the Rosary on my heart. I was not sharing it, though, and so I was crucifying Him. With this knowledge, I was moved—shook—beyond words, and a sadness took hold of me. It was a sadness that prompted me to make this book a top priority.

Now is the time. The world currently is simmering with animosity, about to boil over into World War III. Now is the time to take seriously the message of Fatima (more about that later) and the plea for a Rosary revival. Make no mistake, if you are reading this, you have been called into this battle for peace. Your service is requested in the army of God. There's a weapon with your name on it.

The issue, therefore, is not about when I decided to write this, but rather, when you will decide to read it, and take it to heart.

"**_Today_**, if you hear His voice, harden not your heart." (Hebrews 3:15)

The time is now, friend. Now is the time. So without further delay, let's explore the mystery of the most powerful prayer on earth (next to the Holy Mass, of course).

Table of Contents

PART 5: HOW

CHAPTER ONE:

The Most Complete Prayer:
The Different Parts to It

In the exercise world, most would agree that it's important to strengthen all parts of the body. Those who focus on lifting weights with just one side of the body, or focus on lifting with just their arms (and neglect their legs or their core) end up with disproportioned strength. Then there are those who only lift weights and never run or walk, or do any type of cardio. This still leaves the person disproportioned in overall fitness.

Exercise is a foundational component to the health of the body because it's what makes the muscles strong enough to perform in life, to be productive. So, it's important that the exercise routine is "complete" and encompasses all parts.

In the spiritual world, our "exercise" is our prayer life. Prayer is a foundational component to the health of the soul, because the grace we receive in prayer is what makes the soul strong enough to perform virtue in life, to become holy.

So, it's important that our prayer life is "complete." It's important that our routine is not focused on just one thing (on *just* petition or *just* praise), lest we become spiritually disproportioned (strong in praise when things are going well, but weak in trust when things are going bad. Or strong in asking for things when in need, but weak in giving thanks when things are received.)

For prayer to be "complete" it must be all-encompassing. The prayer of the Rosary encompasses all types of prayer, and involves all parts of the human person (mind, body, soul). But before we get too far into its fullness, let's look at its components.

If you look at a Rosary you will notice that there are many beads that look the same and other beads that look different. Each bead represents a prayer (or in some cases multiple prayers.) The diagram on the next page illustrates which prayers are prayed on which beads.

Chapter ten on page 112 goes over this in more detail.

The Rosary

⬤ Our Father

⬤ Hail Mary

✝ Apostles Creed

⑩ Hail Mary, Gloria, and Fatima prayer

① Mystery and then a Hail Mary

Now, before you panic looking at all these beads, understand it is not as difficult as it looks. Even though there are 60 beads on a Rosary, there are not 60 *different* prayers. In fact, there are only about seven prayers. So, while it might seem complicated and confusing, the Rosary is mostly repetition. (There's a reason for this, that I will get into later.)

The Rosary starts by praying the Apostle's Creed on the cross. You then pray one "Our Father" and three "Hail Mary's" (for the gift of faith, hope and love).

If you notice, the rest of the Rosary is arranged in five groups, called "decades." Ten smaller, similar beads are separated by a different or larger bead. Each decade starts by praying the "Our Father" on the larger bead, followed by ten "Hail Mary's" on the smaller beads.

After praying the last Hail Mary in a decade, you pray one "Glory Be" and one "Fatima Prayer," though there are no beads to represent these two prayers. They are just prayed on the 10th Hail Mary bead.

So, one decade looks like this: one "Our Father" > ten "Hail Mary's" > one "Glory Be" > one "Fatima Prayer." This pattern is then repeated four more times on the remaining beads.

At this point you may be wondering how something with so much repetition could possibly be so powerful. I will get into this over the next several chapters, but please know this seemingly simple string of prayers is chocked full of Divine mystery.

Some of you (especially those who are Protestant) might also be wondering how fifty Hail Mary's could possibly be pleasing to God, since it seems blasphemous to pray to the Virgin Mary. This, too, will be covered in depth in upcoming chapters. For now, though, I ask you to be patient and bear with me... and to trust me when I tell you it is not at all what you think it is.

Here, now, it is important to note that each decade of the Rosary coincides with a "mystery." A mystery is an event (usually recorded in Scripture) that you meditate on while praying the prayers for that decade. Essentially, as you pray one Our Father and ten Hail Mary's you meditate on one Scriptural event. Praying five decades, you meditate on five different events.

Some of my friends, who have never prayed the Rosary before, might be thinking this sounds like a very "rigid" way to pray. Some prefer more spontaneous, free-flowing prayer in the Spirit. And this is what I love about these friends. But don't discount the Rosary just yet. Again, I assure you, it is not what you think it is. I will get into this in detail in the next couple of chapters.

For now, let me just say this is a format. Books have a format with chapters and subchapters and pages, but the content within that format is rich and varies. Different books take people to different places, feeds people different things, evokes different emotions, speaks to them on different levels. But they all pretty much have the same format.

The Rosary has a format, yes, with decades and prayers and meditations. But the beauty available is rich and varies. There are different mysteries on different days, prayed by different people at different places in their spirituality. The Rosary feeds them different graces, evokes different revelations, speaks on different levels. No two Rosaries are the same, like no two books are the same.

In my opinion, there are seven things that make a prayer a *good* prayer. These are: faith, the Will of God, the power of the Holy Spirit, praise and thanks, repentance, meditation, and Scripture. For example, a prayer of praise and thanks is a good prayer. A prayer that includes Scripture is a good prayer, and so forth and so on. A prayer that has *all seven* of these would not be a good prayer but a great—if not perfect— prayer. It would be a complete prayer. The Rosary has all seven of these things.

1.   ***A complete prayer must have faith.*** In Matthew 9, Jesus cured a hemorrhaging woman and then told her, "thy faith has made you well." In that same chapter, before He healed a blind man, Jesus asked him, "Do you believe?" Mark chapter six says Jesus "was not able to perform any mighty deed there... He was amazed at their lack of faith." He also said pointedly, "Whatever you ask for in prayer with faith, you will receive." (Matthew 21:22)

Through these and other Scriptures, we see that it is our *faith* that unleashes God's power in our lives. For this reason, the Rosary begins with the Apostle's Creed. With this prayer, we answer the question Jesus asked the blind man, "Do you believe?" Through the words of the Creed we respond with a resounding, yes. We proclaim in detail, "I believe in God the Father Almighty...and in Jesus Christ His only Son, Our Lord...I believe in the Holy Spirit..." We confess that we believe in the Trinity and the Truths of the Church, and we set the stage for miracles to come. Unfortunately, some hurry through the Creed as if it is an insignificant prayer. What they fail to realize is the proclamation we make in the Creed is what determines how well the rest of our prayers are heard and answered. Make sure when you pray the Creed to think of every word, carefully, and mean them as you say them.

2.   *A complete prayer must be aligned with God's Will.* The Bible says, "And we have this confidence in him, that if we ask anything according to His will, He hears us." (1John 5:14) Jesus confirmed this when He said, "seek first the kingdom [of God] and his righteousness, and all these things will be given you..." (Matthew 6:33) For this reason, the Rosary contains the Our Father, which says, "thy kingdom come, thy will be done." I will talk much more about this in the next chapter but here it's just important to understand that the Our Father is the full embodiment of the Father's Will for us.

3.   *A complete prayer is prayed in communion with the Holy Spirit.* While praying the Hail Mary, we pray with Jesus' Mother, just like the apostles did on that first Pentecost. As the Bible recalls, "When they entered the city they went to the upper room where they were staying, Peter and John and James and Andrew, Philip and Thomas, Bartholomew and

Matthew, James son of Alphaeus, Simon the Zealot, and Judas son of James. All these devoted themselves with one accord to prayer, together with some women, and Mary the mother of Jesus..." (Acts 1:13-14)

Like the apostles, we pray with Mary, the *Spouse* of the Holy Spirit. The angel Gabriel confirmed this espousal in the Gospel of Luke 1:35, when he said to Mary, "the holy Spirit will come upon you, and the power of the Most High will overshadow you. Therefore, the child to be born will be called holy, the Son of God." The key words here are "over shadow you," meaning "never to leave you." The Holy Spirit did not impregnate Mary and then abandon her. He joined with Her more powerfully and completely than He would any other creature.

Like the apostles, we pray with the Spouse of the Spirit, the Mother of the Son. When we pray the Hail Mary, we enter the Pentecost story, and we can expect the same outpouring and power to descend upon us.

4.   *A complete prayer gives praise and thanks to God.* Psalm 92:2 states, "It is good to give thanks to the Lord, to sing praise to your name, Most High..." And Hebrews 13:15 says, "let us continually offer up a sacrifice of praise to God..." In 1 Thessalonians we are told, "in everything give thanks; for this is God's will for you..." (1 Thess. 5:17-18)

For this reason, the Rosary also contains the "Gloria" prayer which is a doxology – an expression of praise to God. At the end of each decade (after praying in the Spirit with the Mother of God, while meditating on a mystery of faith) we give glory and praise to the Trinity for the fruits of that mystery, which shows we are thankful also.

5.   *A complete prayer moves us to repentance.*
The Bible is clear about how important repentance is. Revelations 2:5 says, "Realize how far you have fallen. Repent... Otherwise, I will come to you and remove your lampstand from its place, unless you repent." He is clear that if we do not repent, He will remove the light from within us. Romans 2:5 also says, "By your stubbornness and [unrepentant] heart, you are storing up wrath for yourself..." Not only will we lose our light, we will incur wrath. In Ezekiel, the Lord said, "Repent and turn away from all your transgressions, so that iniquity may not become a stumbling block to you...repent and live." (Ez. 18:30-32) Here we see that the sins that are not repented block us from making progress in the spiritual life. Whereas repentance leads to life.

These and many other Scriptures show us the importance of repentance. Repentance can literally be the difference between life and death. What's more, repentance shows humility. Why is this important? James 4:10 says, "Humble yourselves before the Lord and he will exalt you." Earlier, in James 4:6, it says, "God opposes the proud." Friends, if you cannot repent, then you do not have humility, which is because of pride. Based on this verse, a prayer that is not humble, is a prayer that God opposes, because there is no middle ground.

So, it is important that our prayer be humble and move us to repentance, which the Rosary does. The Rosary contains the Fatima prayer at the end of each decade, where we pray that the Lord will, "forgives us our sins, and saves us from the fires of Hell."

6.   *A complete prayer includes meditation on the life of Christ.* The Psalms are chocked full of instances that tell of the importance of meditation. The very first one, for example, says, "How blessed is the man who... delights in the law of the LORD, and on His law he meditates day and night." (Psalm 1:1-3) The book of Joshua states, "This book of the law shall not depart from your mouth, but you shall meditate on it day and night... then you will make your way prosperous, and then you will have success." (Joshua 1:8) This is confirmed again in the New Testament where it says, "whatever is true, whatever is honorable, whatever is just, whatever is pure, whatever is lovely, whatever is gracious, if there is any excellence and if there is anything worthy of praise, think about these things... Then the God of peace will be with you." (Philippians 4:8-9)

In these Scriptures alone, we see that meditation on God, His Law, and the things of God enables blessing, prosperity, success, and peace. What's more, Jesus commanded us to "Follow Him." (Mark 2:14) But how can we follow someone we never study? How can we become more like someone we never look at?

For this reason, we meditate on the life of Jesus and Mary when we pray the Rosary. I will talk much more about this in future chapters, but for now it is important to note that, through twenty different mysteries, we are able to meditate on the entirety of Jesus' life – his birth, ministry, death and resurrection.

7.   *A complete prayer includes Scripture.* Scripture is the Word of God, unchanging and relevant for all people of all times. It is power and life. Hebrews 4:12 says, "Indeed, the word of God is living and effective, sharper than any two-edged sword, penetrating even between soul and spirit, joints and marrow, and able to discern reflections and thoughts of the heart."

2 Timothy 3:16 says, "All scripture is inspired by God and is useful for teaching, for refutation, for correction, and for training in righteousness..." Psalm 119:105 says the Word of God is, "a lamp for my feet, a light for my path."

What's more, St. Paul says the Word of God is, "the sword of the Spirit," in Ephesians 6:17. Think about this. A sword is a weapon used against an enemy. In the spiritual sense, our enemy is Satan. Satan isn't afraid of our words, but he is afraid of God's Word.

For this reason, the Rosary contains Scripture, and lots of it. Not only are most of the mysteries events recorded in Scripture, but most of the prayers themselves are found in Scripture also. The Our Father was given to us by Jesus Himself in Matthew 6:9-15. The words of the Hail Mary are also in Scripture in Luke 1:28 and 1:42.

The Rosary, prayed with a right heart, contains all the important aspects that make prayer powerful and effective. Most other prayers contain one or two of these. But the Rosary contains all of them. So it is the most complete prayer. I challenge you to find another prayer that contains this depth, or that accomplishes all that the Rosary does.

CHAPTER TWO:

The Most Powerful Prayer:
The Meaning Behind It

If a student takes an exam and is asked to write an essay using an introductory paragraph, three body paragraphs, and a concluding paragraph—if he or she answers who, what, when, where, why—and completes the essay with each of these things, does that alone ensure it will be the best essay in the class? No. The "completeness" is worth something for the grade, yes. It does help communicate the point in a logical and fluid way. But the words themselves, and their _meaning_, are what make the paragraphs a powerful essay.

Such is the case with the Rosary. The Rosary has all the different components to make it the most complete prayer. You would think this would also make it the most powerful prayer. And, to some degree, you would be right in thinking so. But, this really only scratches the surface. Like an essay, the power of the Rosary is not merely in its format or its completeness, but also in its meaning and depth (and its Author which I will get into later). To discover its true power, we need to look at the actual words of the prayers—specifically the Our Father and Hail Mary.

These prayers are familiar to most Catholics. They're often taught to kids in their earliest ages. While this is good, I think that because they are memorized, they sometimes become a little "too familiar." Over the course of time, they can somehow lose their luster if you will. They can become words that are just rattled off from memory, instead of prayers actually prayed from the heart.

For this reason, I would like to go through the actual words to these prayers (and their meaning) in the hopes that we can rediscover their beauty and depth... in the hopes that we can see them in new ways, and in turn, come to understand the grandeur and power of the Rosary because of them.

OUR FATHER

Our Father, who art in Heaven,
Hallowed be Thy Name.
Thy Kingdom come, Thy Will be done,
On Earth as it is in Heaven.
Give us this day, our daily bread.
And forgive us our trespasses,
As we forgive those who trespass against us.
And lead us not into temptation,
But deliver us from evil. Amen.

This prayer was dictated word-for-word by Jesus Himself, and recorded in Scripture as the Living Word of God (Mt 6:9-13). It is, therefore, packed full of rich, divine meaning. (Would you expect anything less from a prayer penned by the hand of Almighty God?) From the lips of Jesus, this is directed to God the Father, and it contains seven different petitions. This is significant.

Proverbs 24:16 says that a just man falls _seven_ times. And there are _seven_ petitions in the Our Father. So, according to St. Augustine—bishop and Doctor of the Church—whenever we say the Our Father _devoutly_ our venial sins are forgiven. Yes, forgiven. Now, let's go through it line by line.

"Our Father,"

By addressing God as our "Father," we call Him by the same name Jesus called Him, thus declaring we are Jesus' brothers and sisters—as well as brothers and sisters of those who also call Him Father. With this one, little line we state that we belong to the family of God. By stating who He is (Father), we also state who we are (His children).

"Who art in Heaven,"

By saying "Who art in Heaven," we acknowledge our true home—where we come from and where we are going. If our Father lives in Heaven, then so should His children, right? With this line, we state our desire to be with Him for all eternity. By stating where He is (Heaven), we state where we want to be (with Him in Heaven forever).

"Hallowed be Thy Name."

The word "hallowed" means holy. This line essentially says, "holy is Your Name." If the Name of God is Holy, and God is our Father, then shouldn't His children bear the same name? On earth we often take our biological Father's last name in order to associate ourselves with him. Likewise, our Heavenly Father's Name is Holy... and since we have already declared that we are His children, we must take His name too. We must become holy. By stating what He is (holy), we state what we want to become (holy, just like Him).

"Thy Kingdom come,"

Up until this point, the words of the Our Father are addressing God, like a salutation in a letter. With this salute we reveal who He is, and also who we are in Him. Here, though, we begin the seven petitions that St. Augustine talked about. First, we petition "His Kingdom come."

God is not just a Father, He is a King, with a Kingdom. He is royalty... and therefore, so are we. The problem is, we are like the prodigal son in Luke 15:11-32. In many ways, we have disobeyed our Father. Through sin, we have left His Kingdom (the city of God), and have been living precariously in the city of man. But, with this line, we state our desire to return to Him and live in His Kingdom. This is different from the earlier line, where we said we want to live with Him in Heaven.

Many people assume this means "Thy Kingdom come upon earth," as if we are praying for the coming of that end-time, where all nations of the earth will be under God's dominion and He will reign supreme. And yes, we can expect that to take place at some point, but, "thy kingdom come" in this prayer means something a little more intimate, I think.

Here we are praying for the spiritual Kingdom of God to come down into our hearts. We are praying for the

Kingdom that Jesus said, "was at hand" two thousand years ago. (Mt. 4:17 and 10:7) Clearly, this was not a physical, earthly Kingdom. Rather, Jesus confirmed, "The coming of the kingdom of God cannot be observed…For behold, the kingdom of God is among you." (Luke17:20-21)

We are praying for the Kingdom to come within us… for the Holy Trinity to dwell in our hearts. And here's the thing: when each heart bears the fullness of God within them, _that_ is when the earth will be under God's dominion. That is how His reign on earth will take place—one heart at a time, starting with ourselves. (For more information on this, and how to accomplish this, I wrote a do-it-yourself retreat called "Victory in the Spiritual Garden" to help you draw closer to God within. It is currently available on Amazon.)

"Thy Kingdom come" is basically our main intention with this prayer. If there was a line to be highlighted, underlined, circled… this would be it. This is the focal point, the main gist of this prayer. The first lines leading up to it preface what or who's Kingdom (God's). All the lines following it, describe how it will take place. So, let's continue.

"Thy Will be done, on earth as it is in Heaven."

The question now is: _how_ can this Kingdom come into our hearts? First and foremost, by doing God's Will on earth, just as it is done by the Saints and Angels in Heaven. And what is God's Will? His Will is to live according to the commandments, yes. But it's much simpler than that even. His Will is to love God above all else and to love your neighbor as yourself, as Jesus explained in the Gospel of Matthew. (Mt. 22:37-39) If we can accomplish this with every thought, word and action, then His Will *can* be done here on earth as it is done in Heaven.

"Give us this day, our daily bread."

How can we make sure we love God above all else and neighbor as our self? To do this in every thought, word, and action in every moment of every day is no doubt a difficult task. But, this line of the prayer tells us how it can be done. We ask for God to give us grace (or "bread") for the day. We ask for His strength, His wisdom, His instruction. Jesus said, "One does not live by bread alone, but by every word that comes forth from the mouth of God." (Mt.4:4)

With this line, we admit that we cannot do this on our own, and that we need God's assistance, His grace. It also alludes to the mystery of the Eucharist—the bread of angels, His Real Presence—which provides more grace to our souls than anything else we could ever do in this life.

"And forgive us our trespasses,"

What is one way to ensure we receive this grace? To make sure there is nothing in our life that could block us from receiving it. And yes, you guessed it, this line of the prayer explains how.

Grace is given to us freely, from God, as long as we are in a state of grace—meaning as long as we are not living in mortal (serious) sin. So, we receive grace through regular Confession, through "forgiveness of our trespasses." Mortal sin can be like a wall, preventing us from receiving the grace we need to do God's Will and fully experience the Kingdom. But the mercy of God breaks down that wall so His sanctifying grace then floods our souls.

"As we forgive those who trespass against us,"

When we confess our sins, how can we make sure God forgives us? We are forgiven according to how we forgive others who trespass against us (as well as how we forgive ourselves). This is important because unforgiveness can also be a wall blocking grace.

"And lead us not into temptation,"

How do we make sure we stay free from unforgiveness and/or mortal sin? We ask God not to lead us into the temptation to commit mortal sin, or to be unloving towards our neighbor. We recognize we are weak, and we have a tendency to sin, so we humbly ask God to keep us away from these occasions and to prevent us from entering tempting situations. Like Jesus said in Scripture, "If your hand causes you to sin, cut it off." (Mk. 9:43)

"But deliver us from evil. Amen."

The last line of the prayer takes it even a step further. Previously, we asked God to not lead us into temptation with people, places, things, behaviors—tangible things of the earth. Now, we ask him to deliver us from spiritual temptations—the attacks from the evil one, things we cannot see or touch or hear with our ears, but those things that tempt us nonetheless.

As you can see, the Our Father moves backwards from the main, highlighted intention: "Thy Kingdom come." Each line after that reveals a little bit more about how this will come about. If you reverse the prayer, you see the journey moving forward from where we are now.

For example, we ask God to protect us from the devil and from temptation, so that we can be free of unforgiveness when we confess our sins, to receive grace, to do God's Will, to inherit the Kingdom.

The Our Father prayer is basically the summation of the soul's spiritual journey. We petition our needs for every step of the journey, until we arrive at complete unity with God, when His Kingdom is thriving within us. Essentially, with the Our Father, we are praying for our sanctification.

As I mentioned last chapter, we start with faith, by saying, "I believe" in the creed. Then, we state our intention with the Our Father. Though, technically, we state _seven_ very big and worthy and pleasing intentions. But it doesn't end there. Next, we pray the Hail Mary.

HAIL MARY

Hail Mary, full of grace,
The Lord is with Thee.
Blessed art Thou among women
And blessed is the fruit of Thy womb, Jesus.

Holy Mary, Mother of God,
Pray for us sinners,
Now and at the hour of our death. Amen.

The Hail Mary is a short, little prayer that I could write an entire book on, by itself. I will do my best, though, to summarize the enormity I feel in my heart so as to stay on track.

"Hail Mary, full of grace, the Lord is with Thee."

Like the Our Father, the Hail Mary begins with a salutation... this time, though, to the Blessed Virgin Mary, not God. Right here, from the get-go, is where many people develop problems with this prayer. They argue that prayer is to be directed to God alone, and that praying to the Virgin Mary (who is a creature), is simply idolatry. On the surface, I get their argument. If you do not understand this prayer, then yes, I suppose it could "seem" that way. But let's look a little deeper.

First, it is important to note that the word "hail" in the Bible is a greeting of joy and peace, which was a common salutation in those days. "Hail" is not a greeting that somehow elevates Mary to a Godly status. Second, we must remember these words are *Scripture*. In the Gospel of Luke (1:28), the angel Gabriel appears to Mary and says, "Hail, favored one! The Lord is with you." Then the angel said to her, "Do not be afraid, Mary, for you have found favor with God." (Luke 1:30)

From these verses, we see that these are not the made-up words of Catholics who decided to write an idolatrous prayer. These are the words of an archangel—a messenger of God—recorded in the very Word of God. So, to have issues with the beginning of the Hail Mary... well, quite frankly, is to have issues with Scripture, or even angels.

Not only that, these words are power. These words are like the horn preceding and announcing the arrival of a King. This angelic salutation, "Hail Mary full of grace," was THE moment, friends—the moment that all the angels in Heaven, and all the prophets of old, had waited and hoped and longed for. This was _the_ moment that would fulfill age-old prophesies, and change the future for all of mankind. This was the moment of the beginning. The moment that would set into motion the coming of the Savior, the defeat of the devil, the opening of the gates of Heaven. Oh friends, these words are not idolatrous, they are blessed, holy, miraculous, and very powerful.

St Louis de Montfort said, "The greatest event in the whole history of the world was the incarnation of the Eternal Word by whom the world was redeemed, and peace was restored between God and men." He also said, because of this, these words in the salutation, "terrify devils and put them to shame." [1]

Think about it. It was essentially from these words (and the consent given after) that God saved the world, because it is from these words that He came down from

---

[1] _"The Secret of The Rosary"_ by Saint Louis de Montfort, 1993 TAN Books, #45

Heaven, entered the womb of a virgin, and thereby sanctified mankind. And, it is by these same words—uttered from the mouths of those praying the rosary—that He will once again save the world. But I will talk more about this is later chapters.

Despite of the obvious power in the angelic salutation, some people still argue that God would prefer to hear a prayer directed to His Name, rather than the name of a creature. But, actually, I think He delights in the reminiscing.

My husband and I sometimes repeat words that our kids used to say when they were young... sometimes they are comical phrases, sometimes they are sweet and endearing. But we remember each of them with a warm smile. Somehow, uttering those words of long ago makes it present again, at least for a moment. With those words, I can almost see my daughter's tiny face, and hear her squeaky voice once again. And because of that, my heart soars as if it's the first time I've heard it.

I believe this is what happens with God, when we repeat the words, "Hail Mary, full of grace." I imagine it brings to the Father's mind that moment, the excitement, and the joy of witnessing Mary's surprise, and then the faith-filled fiat She gave His messenger. I imagine the Son of God, who was to take His place in her womb, remembers these words just as fondly. It is likely a reminder of the eagerness of being welcomed and the anticipation of humanity being saved. I imagine the Holy Spirit, who espoused Himself to Her, watched the salutation and awaited her "I do" with just as much enthusiasm.

But even the analogy of my husband and I reminiscing does not do this reality justice. I believe that the Triune God, who is not bound to time or space—but who lives fully in the present, who is the great "I am"—I believe He hears these words as if it is _really_ the moment once again. I believe somehow (beyond what we can understand) God relives these words truly, fully, and far more intensely, than my husband and I relive the words of our daughter. And I believe that when we utter the angelic salutation, we are in that moment with God then, too.

What's more, when we say, "Mary full of grace," the key word here is "grace." This signifies that Mary is a creature who has received the grace of God. But this doesn't make it idolatry, it makes it praise. Mary is a creature in whom _God_ has done great things. God is the focal point of this line of prayer, because grace is something given to creatures by God, not something they give to themselves.

The angel said, "Hail! Favored one!" This means _God_ has done this to Her. God elevated Her, favored Her, chose Her. Not Catholics, not people. _God_ did this, for _His_ purposes and the fulfillment of _His_ plan (which was the salvation of mankind). And so, with these words, we give glory to God for that plan.

What glory do we give Him by detesting these words, which announce His plan? What glory do we give Him by resenting the status to which _He_ elevated Her? How does it give glory to God to spurn these words, which are technically _His_ words—words that His messenger obediently carried to Earth from Heaven? Friend, it does not give any glory to God to snub this prayer.

Finally, since these opening words are a greeting to the Blessed Virgin Mary, we can safely assume that She hears us, and that She comes to us at the sound of this greeting. From the onset of this prayer, the Virgin Mary is in our midst. It's not logical to think that we would greet Her kindly, and She would ignore us.

Why is it important if She is in our midst? Because it says, "the Lord is with thee." Where She is, He is. If the angel said, "the Lord is with you" _prior_ to the incarnation of Jesus in Her womb, prior to the Holy Spirit coming upon Her, how much more is the Lord God with Her now, after these events?

At this point in the Rosary, the Father is present in our midst because we have greeted Him in the Our Father, and the Son and the Holy Spirit are present in our midst now because the Blessed Virgin Mary is in our midst and has brought Them to us.

"Blessed art Thou among women, and blessed is the Fruit of Thy womb, Jesus."

For those of you who have a problem with what I said earlier—that the Virgin Mary brings Jesus and the Holy Spirit into our midst—I want to go over the next line of the Hail Mary with you. This line is also in Scripture.

"When Elizabeth heard Mary's greeting, the infant leaped in her womb, and Elizabeth, filled with the Holy

Spirit, cried out in a loud voice and said, 'Most blessed are you among women, and blessed is the fruit of your womb.'" (Luke 1:42)

After the incarnation, Mary visited her pregnant cousin Elizabeth, and upon her arrival Elizabeth immediately recognized the presence of God within Mary. In fact, the Scripture states that at just the _sound_ of Mary's greeting, the baby leaped, and Elizabeth was filled with the Holy Spirit. This is substantial.

Remember that when we greet Mary with the words, "Hail Mary," she does not ignore our greeting. Not only does She not ignore it, I believe Mary returns it with a greeting of Her own. This is significant because when the Mother of God and the Spouse of God comes into our midst and greets us in prayer, it can have a powerful effect on us (if we are open). Elizabeth's words in Scripture prove it is true. These words are the proof of what is spiritually taking place as we pray the Rosary.

If we state our intention in the Our Father—to become holy and to inherit the Kingdom—then we need the outpouring of the Holy Spirit to accomplish this. We need to experience what Elizabeth and her baby, John the Baptist, experienced. We need our own visitation of Jesus and Mary, our own Pentecost with the Holy Spirit.

What's more, when we repeat the words of Elizabeth, "Blessed art Thou among women, and blessed is the fruit of your womb, Jesus," we are proclaiming truth. We are proclaiming the Bible to be true. We are proclaiming the incarnation to be true. We are proclaiming the plan of salvation—that "a virgin shall conceive and bear a son" (Is. 7:14)—to be true.

And yes, friends, we are proclaiming that Mary is blessed. The angel calls Her "favored one." She was chosen to be the Mother of the Messiah, overshadowed by the Spirit! That's blessed. And quite frankly, refusing to acknowledge this or withholding honor due Her is dangerous.

We don't hesitate to call popular pastors and speakers blessed because of their spiritual gifts. We don't hesitate to show gratitude to them for the way they make worship services possible, or for the way they grace us with powerful sermons. Why can't we do the same for the Blessed Virgin Mary?

Why can't we acknowledge that Mary's spiritual gift is the single greatest gift ever given to humanity? Why can't we show gratitude for the way She has made it possible for us to worship the Son of God? Friends, there would be no Gospel without the Virgin Mary. That famous pastor or speaker, quoting Jesus in powerful sermons, does so only because the Blessed Virgin Mary brought the Word of God into the world. That is blessed. That deserves honor and gratitude.

"Holy Mary, Mother of God,"

Here is another salutation, and another place where some people get uncomfortable—calling Mary holy. But it's important to understand that Jesus made Her His dwelling place. Therefore, Mary is the new Ark of the New Covenant—which, my friends, *is* holy.

In the Old Testament, the Ark that held the presence of God had to be pure and untouched by sinful human hands. 2 Samuel 6:6-7 says, "Uzzah stretched out his hand to the ark of God and...God struck him on that spot, and he died there in God's presence."

If the old Ark that held the presence of God could not have a trace of sin touch it, then what about the New Ark (the womb of Mary) that held not only His spiritual presence, but His physical body? It's not logical to think that God would come to dwell in the womb of a woman who is NOT holy, when nothing unholy could even touch the first Ark.

Additionally, His Godly presence in Her made her even _more_ holy, even _more_ sacred. She was made sacred in the same way the manger, the tomb, His tunic, and the cross (anything that held Him) were made sacred. But even more so.

She is infinitely more sacred than these because She did not just give Him a resting place or a covering, She gave Him Her body—Her cells, Her genes, Her blood. She gave Him nourishment, protection, care, everything. She gave life to the Author of Life. She is the Mother of God. Think about that.

The term "Mother of God" seems like a contradiction in terms. How can God, who has no beginning, have a mother? It seems like a paradox, but Mary is the mother of Jesus, Jesus is God, and so Mary is the Mother of God.

The real wonderment, though, lies not in Mary, but in Jesus. It's like saying, "the mother of the Pope" or "the mother of the President" or "the mother of a famous person." What makes the mother special is the Pope, the President or the famous person. What makes the "Mother of God" special is God... and because it is God, She is infinitely more special than any other mother—any other human person for that matter.

What's more, the title "Mother of God" says that God chose to step down from Heaven, into Earth. He chose to hide His glory by putting on human flesh. He chose to surrender His power by becoming a helpless baby. It says that divine providence chose to be provided for. The Lord of Hosts chose to be obedient and submissive and dutiful.

The title "Mother of God" speaks of both the self-sacrificing love of God and His great desire to be close to us. It speaks of a God who was not content to watch over us from the Heavens, but who chose to become one of us, for love of us.

"Pray for us sinners,"

The salutation, "holy Mary, Mother of God," petitions not just a woman, but THE woman. The woman who is closer to God than anyone else—because of Her holiness and Her maternity—and who holds more sway with God than anyone else.

If you don't think this is true, I will remind you of the story of the wedding at Cana found in the Gospel of John (2:1-12). They ran out of wine and Mary approached Jesus about it. At this point, Jesus had not worked any miracles. He said to Her, "My time has not yet come." (2:4) But Mary wanted Him to do something to help, and Jesus did. He changed jugs of water into jugs of wine. More miraculously, though, He changed the timeframe of His ministry for Her, and worked His first miracle at Her request.

This is important because when we ask Mary to "pray for us sinners," we can be confident She has great intercessory power. What's more, we can be confident that She is in fact praying.

When Elizabeth greeted Mary at the visitation—when she proclaimed, "Blessed art thou among women and blessed is the fruit of thy womb,"—what did Mary say in reply?

Scripture says that Mary replied, "My soul proclaims the greatness of the Lord," (Luke 1:46). Mary immediately responded to Elizabeth's greeting with praise and thanks to God. She proclaimed the beautiful Magnificat. When we greet Mary with the same words as Elizabeth, I believe Mary does the same. I believe She responds with praise and thanks to God on our behalf.

"Now and at the hour of our death. Amen."

When we greet the Blessed Virgin Mary (the Mother of God and the Spouse of the Holy Spirit) and ask Her to pray for us, She takes a vested interest in us—not just at that moment, but at every moment for the rest of our life, especially at the hour of our death. And this is important.

You see, the moments of our life are not inconsequential. Each moment is like a spiritual coin that we either deposit into a savings of eternal life or a savings of eternal damnation—we either invest each moment into Heaven or Hell. We choose, in each moment, either God or His enemy. Jesus said, "whoever is not with Me is against me." (Mt. 12:30) There is no in between. Each moment, each choice, each word has eternal value that is accounted for on the scale of justice at the end of life.

I believe that the devil comes for what is his in the end. I believe the foothold we give him in life, he uses at the hour of death. He will come with one last temptation, trying to get us to deny Christ and to abandon the faith once and for all.

But the Blessed Virgin Mary has power over the devil. This was foretold in the very beginning in the Garden of Eden when God told the serpent, "I will put enmity between you and the Woman, and between your offspring and Hers. She will crush thy head while you strike at Her heel." (Genesis 3:15)

God Himself placed enmity between them -- between Mary and the devil. God did it. He is the one who involved Mary in the great spiritual battle. Would He have made them enemies and then not equipped Mary to do battle? Of course not. That's just mean. He put them in total opposition of each other and then gave Her power against him.

Because Eve listened to the serpent in the garden and coerced Adam into sin, Mary is the New Eve, who will crush the serpent in the spiritual garden of the human heart and protect men from sin. She was given this power from God Himself. He ordained it at the very beginning. (For more on this read "Victory in the Spiritual Garden" by Stacy Mal.)

So, each Hail Mary that we pray in life—petitioning the chief enemy of Satan—is grace for the moment to resist him. It helps us make deposits into the savings for Heaven, not Hell. In the Our Father we pray that we are not led into temptation, and that we are delivered from all evil—so we can choose better, love better, become holy. Here is how we do that. With the Blessed Virgin Mary.

With each Hail Mary the Mother of God, the Spouse of the Spirit, and the enemy of Satan petitions God on our behalf. It's grace for the moment, but it is also grace stored for the hour of death. Fifty Hail Mary's prayed on one Rosary is like an arsenal stored for the final battle. It's like building a forcefield of protection that will allow us to rest in peace and faith in those last moments. Just think of the strength of the forcefield—the grace accumulated—if we pray a Rosary every day of our life! The devil cannot overtake such a soul.

According to St. Louis de Montfort, "Never will anyone who says his Rosary every day become a formal heretic or be led astray by the devil. This is a statement which I would sign with my blood."[2]

---

[2] "The Secret of The Rosary" by Saint Louis de Montfort, 1993 TAN Books, #78

He continues, "Even if you are on the brink of damnation, even if you have one foot in hell, even if you have sold your soul to the devil as sorcerers do who practice black magic, and even if you are a heretic as obstinate as a devil, sooner or later you will be converted and will amend your life and save your soul, if—and mark well what I say—if you say the Rosary devoutly every day until death for the purpose of knowing the truth and obtaining contrition and pardon for your sins." [3]

The Blessed Virgin Mary confirmed this Herself, in the 1400s, when she told Blessed Alan de la Roche, "Whoever shall persevere in the devotion of the holy Rosary, with its prayers and meditations, shall be rewarded for it; I shall obtain for him full remission of the penalty and the guilt of all his sins at the end of his life. And let this not seem incredible to you. It is easy for me because I am the Mother of the King of Heaven, and He calls me full of grace. And being filled with grace, I am able to dispense it freely to my dear children."[4]

---

[3] Ibid, #4
[4] Ibid #89

CHAPTER THREE:

The Most Productive Prayer:
The Mysteries Within It

Sometimes things aren't always as they appear at first glance. Sometimes you even need to look at it through a different lens if you want to see the truth of a thing. Take for example, human blood. If you were to cut your finger and start bleeding, the blood would look like a stagnant, solid-colored, red substance.

But if you looked at that same blood under a microscope, you would see something entirely different. You would see a landscape of numerous, circular-shaped blood cells, of varying shades, living, moving and coagulating. That one drop of blood, magnified under a lens, would resemble a busy, living environment, almost like that of an ant farm.

Such is the case with the Rosary. At first glance the Rosary (which, yes, is the most complete and powerful prayer) appears to be a vocal prayer—one of repetition, praise, and petition. And this is true. But there is so much more to it than even that. The Rosary is also a contemplative prayer. It contains what are called "mysteries" of the faith—specific events from the lives of Jesus and Mary that we are to meditate on as we pray the decades.

Here, the Rosary (like a drop of blood) becomes so much more when viewed under the lens of faith. Here, we close the eyes of the flesh and begin to "look" at the life of Christ with the eyes of the soul. And just like the lens of a microscope, the Spirit of God magnifies these moments and brings them to life for us.

In meditation we begin to see that Jesus is not a stagnant image. He is not a statue, or a man from long ago. Rather, He is a living, moving being in the here and now. Like blood is for the human body, these meditations are the lifeforce of the Rosary. Through them, we not only come to see and understand Jesus differently, but we come to see and understand ourselves differently also. And this is where transformation takes place. This is what makes the Rosary so productive and fruitful. Meditation and reflection is the key to change.

If our intention, as we say in the Our Father, is to become holy like God is holy, then we learn to do this by studying Him in meditation. We must ponder the Son of God, Jesus Christ, who told us to "follow Him." (Mt. 16:24) The student must watch the teacher.

St. Gregory of Nyssa made this comparison: "We are all artists and our souls are all blank canvasses which we have to fill in. The colors which we use are the Christian virtues, and the original which we have to copy is Jesus Christ, the perfect living image of God the Father. Just as a painter who wants to do a life-like portrait places the model before his eyes and looks at it before making each stroke, so the Christian must always have before his eyes the life and virtues of Jesus Christ, so as never to say, think or do anything which is not in conformity with his model." [5]

In meditation we become like soft clay in the Hand of the Potter. The Holy Spirit (Who is espoused to the Blessed Virgin Mary, and Who is in our midst as we pray the Hail Mary), is using us and forming us according the model that have set our sights on in the mysteries.

Now, perhaps you are wondering, *"Which is it? Do I focus on the words of the Hail Mary as I pray them, or do I focus on the meditation for that decade?"* Well, both. I would let the Spirit of God lead you in that regard. But I would start by focusing on the meditation.

Have you ever started singing a song and then got lost in thought while singing? Perhaps it was a hymn or worship song? Perhaps it was the song that you and your spouse danced to at your wedding? Perhaps it was a song from your first concert? Have you ever sung the lyrics while your mind thought of some other event or person? That familiar song puts us in a mood and brings us into another reality. It sets the stage for our thinking, but it's not the actual lyrics that we are thinking about.

This is what often takes place during the Rosary. The repetition of the Hail Mary serves as the melody of our prayer—our words mixed with the canticle of Mary, the Magnificat She sings to God as we pray. This harmony brings us into the presence of the Trinity and sets the stage for our meditation. But it's the mysteries that we

---

[5] *"The Secret of The Rosary"* by Saint Louis de Montfort, 1993 TAN Books #65

actually think about. It's like the bride who sings her wedding song while thinking about the dance with her spouse.

That is not to say the Hail Mary shouldn't be considered important or that we should hurry through it disrespectfully. As we already proved in the chapter before this, the Hail Mary is of GREAT importance and therefore should be prayed with great reverence. The Mother of God and the vessel of our salvation also deserves to be greeted with honor and respect. But it is not as crucial to meditate on the words of the Hail Mary fifty times over, as it is to meditate on the different moments in life of Christ. We focus on the mysteries like a flame that devours a log, while our faith, love and understanding of the prayers ascend from our hearts like smoke.

I used the analogy of a song earlier, because that is precisely what the Rosary is supposed to emulate. The original Rosary consisted of fifteen decades—150 Hail Mary's—which is the same number as there are psalms in the Book of the Psalms of David.

The 150 Davidic Psalms (known as the Psalter of David) was prayed by Old Testament Israel and was later chanted by early Christian monks. Lay Christians who did not have copies of Scripture, or who could not devote the time to such a practice, were unable to adopt this for their own use. So, they began to substitute 150 Our Fathers, and then later 150 Hail Mary's, for the 150 Psalms. This became known as the

Psalter of the Blessed Virgin Mary and eventually was called the Rosary.

The Rosary was then divided up. The fifteen decades were divided into three groups—the Joyful Mysteries (meditations on the life of Jesus), the Sorrowful Mysteries (meditations on the death of Jesus), and the Glorious Mysteries (meditations on the victory of Jesus). Today, each group contains five decades (50 Hail Mary's) and is prayed on a different day of the week so that by the week's end, the entire Psalter is prayed, and the entire life, death, and glory of Jesus is pondered.

In 2002, Pope John Paul II (Saint John Paul the Great) added a new group of mysteries to the Rosary—the Luminous Mysteries—which focus on the public ministry of Jesus. The pope felt there was a gap in the meditations, since the Joyful Mysteries only focus on Jesus' birth and childhood.

It's important to note, too, that the 150 psalms of David *prefigure* the Rosary. It is the "new song," prophesied of. (Ps.98) And according to St. Louis de Montfort, the Rosary surpasses the psalms because if the psalms sing of the One who is to come, the Rosary proclaims Him as having come. St. Louis said, "The [Rosary] bears a nobler fruit, that of the Word incarnate, whereas David's Psalter only prophesies His coming. Two, just as the real thing is more important than its prefiguration and the body surpasses the shadow, so the Psalter of our Lady is greater than David's Psalter, which did no more than prefigure it." [6]

Blessed Albert the Great, who had St. Thomas Aquinas as his student, said that it was the mysteries of the Rosary that gave it nobility. He said that by simply, "thinking of or meditating on the passion of Jesus Christ a Christian gains more merit than if he had fasted on bread and water every Friday for a year...or had recited the whole Book of Psalms every day." [7] Think, then, how great the merit of the Rosary must be, which calls to mind the whole life, ministry, death and glory of the Lord.

I will include reflections later in chapter 11, but for now, let's just look at what the mysteries are.

The Joyful Mysteries

The five Joyful Mysteries of the Rosary, which are prayed on Mondays and Saturdays, call to mind specific moments from the early life of Jesus and Mary, namely His conception, birth and childhood. Through these mysteries, we ponder the love of God shown in the fact that He put on flesh and became a helpless baby.

The Joyful Mysteries are:

1. The Annunciation: the angel Gabriel appears to Mary, and Jesus is conceived in Her womb.

---

[6] *"The Secret of The Rosary"* by Saint Louis de Montfort, 1993 TAN Books #22
[7] Ibid, #88

2. The Visitation: Mary visits her cousin Elizabeth who is pregnant with John the Baptist.
3. The Nativity: Jesus is born in a stable in Bethlehem.
4. The Presentation: Mary and Joseph present the baby Jesus in the Temple, and are met by Simeon and Anna.
5. The Finding of Jesus in the Temple: Mary and Joseph lose the child Jesus while in Jerusalem, but later find Him in the temple.

The Sorrowful Mysteries

The five Sorrowful Mysteries of the Rosary, which are prayed on Tuesdays and Fridays, call to mind the Passion and death of Jesus. Through these mysteries, we ponder the mercy of God shown in the sufferings He underwent for our sake.

The Sorrowful Mysteries are:

1. The Agony in the Garden: The night before His death, Jesus suffers anxiety and sweats blood.
2. The Scourging at the Pillar: Jesus is scourged by Roman soldiers.
3. The Crowning with Thorns: Jesus is mockingly clothed with a cloak and crowned with thorny branches.
4. The Carrying of the Cross: Jesus is forced to carry a Cross upon His back to the hill where He is crucified.

5. The Crucifixion: Jesus is nailed to His Cross and
    dies.

The Glorious Mysteries

The five Glorious Mysteries of the Rosary, which are
prayed on Wednesdays and Sundays, call to mind the
victory of Jesus and Mary. Through these mysteries, we
ponder their triumph over satan, sin and death.

The Glorious Mysteries are:

1. The Resurrection: Jesus rises from the dead and
    leaves the burial tomb.
2. The Ascension: After forty days on earth, Jesus
    ascends to Heaven to be with His Father.
3. The Descent of the Holy Spirit: The Holy Spirit
    comes upon the disciples who are gathered in
    prayer with Mary.
4. The Assumption of the Blessed Virgin Mary: The
    body of Mary is taken up to Heaven and
    reunited with Her Son.
5. The Coronation of the Blessed Virgin Mary:
    Mary is crowned Queen of Heaven next to Her
    Son, who is King of Heaven.

The Luminous Mysteries

The five Luminous Mysteries of the Rosary, which are
prayed on Thursdays, call to mind the public ministry of

Jesus. Through these mysteries, we ponder His preaching, teaching, and work.

The Luminous Mysteries are:

1. The Baptism in the Jordan: John the Baptist baptizes Jesus in the River Jordan.
2. The Wedding at Cana: At Mary's request, Jesus changes water into wine at a wedding feast.
3. The Proclamation of the Kingdom: Jesus proclaims the Kingdom of God is at hand.
4. The Transfiguration: The appearance of Jesus changes to bright light, and Peter, James, and John see Him talking to Moses and Elijah.
5. The Institution of the Holy Eucharist: Jesus conducts the Last Supper with His apostles, where He gives them the first Eucharist.

Through these four sets of mysteries, we do not just consider one aspect of His life. Rather, we ponder the *fullness* of God. And because God is not bound to time and space, we actually enter these mysteries spiritually, through our meditation. We make ourselves present in the Gospel story. We live His childhood, His ministry, His death, and His glory with Him... and we receive the grace He procured for us in each of these moments. This produces enormous effects in our souls.

In fact, St. Louis de Montfort said, "You can be sure that, while you are meditating on these mysteries and honoring them, Jesus will show His sacred wounds to

His Father in Heaven. He will plead for you and obtain for you contrition and the forgiveness of your sins." [8]

---

[8] *"The Secret of The Rosary"* by Saint Louis de Montfort, 1993 TAN Books, #83

CHAPTER FOUR:

Our Lady of the Rosary and Her Preachers

Picture it. A young 14 year old girl is minding her own business in prayer, when bam! An angel appears and tells Her She has been chosen by God to have a baby—and not just any baby, but the Messiah. Life changes in an instant. She is chosen by God for a seemingly impossible task. A task that few people could believe or understand. A task that risks her reputation (a virgin pregnant?) and threatens her closest relationships. But she agrees to the pregnancy anyway.

At first, she is misunderstood by Joseph, her fiancé. He considers abandoning her, because he assumes She has been unfaithful. This pierces Her heart because She knows She hasn't done anything wrong.

At this point in the Gospel story you feel bad for Mary. You want to just shout, "She's telling the truth! Listen to Her!" Then, an angel appears to Joseph in a dream and reveals the truth about the baby. He believes, and the good Joseph devotes himself to Her. He also accepts his own role in this unbelievable calling.

Whew! You can relax now.

Or can you?

What if I told you the same thing is still happening now? What if I told you Mary is still misunderstood, still at risk for abandonment, still pierced? Not by Joseph, but by all those who do not believe in the other part of Her calling.

Mary was chosen to be the Mother of God, yes. But, She was also chosen to be the Mother of All the Living—the mother of all the brothers and sisters of Christ, Her Son. That means you and me. She was chosen to bring Him into the world, and to bring us out of it; chosen to physically raise Him and to spiritually raise us. Jesus called Her to this while He was on the Cross, just before He died. (John 19:27) And She accepted.

She accepted a call that would last until the end of the world, until the last brothers and sisters of Christ make it safely into eternity. For this reason, the Virgin Mary has been appearing across the globe to countless visionaries since around 40 A.D. She appears in sun-like radiance, bestowing love and peace, urging people to return to God... teaching them, encouraging them, mothering them.

To some this sounds preposterous—the idea of visions and apparitions. But the Bible filled with apparition accounts. They are described in the book of Ezekiel (40:3), the book of Daniel (8:15 and 10:4), and 1 Samuel (28:12), to name a few. Moses and Elijah even appeared on Mount Tabor with Jesus at the Transfiguration (Luke 9:28-36). So apparitions are not preposterous—not if you believe in the Bible.

In fact, many of the apparitions of the Virgin Mary have been judged "worthy of belief" by ecclesiastical authorities; several have also been validated by Eastern or Oriental Orthodox authorities; and many others were accepted by the undivided Church. [9]

Science, too, has acknowledged that a phenomenon is in fact taking place. Medical experts have verified physical healings, unexplainable by other means. And wayward societies, such as Mexico in the early 1500s, have experienced surges of Christian conversion (8 million Aztec people in that instance alone). The Mother of God has left her mark in the lands of Hindus, Jews, Moslems, Protestants, Catholics, and Orthodox, Buddhists and Shintoists, Confucians and Communists, and Aztecs and animists. [10]

Despite all this, many people still do not believe She has appeared or that She was chosen for this task—to lead us back to God. So, Her reputation suffers, as do Her relationships with those She dearly loves. It seems as though, for a time, history is repeating itself. What Mary suffered while bringing Jesus to us, she suffers now again, bringing us to Him. And sometimes, as I watch it take place, I just want to shout, "She's telling the truth! Listen to Her!"

For this reason, I would like to spend this chapter talking a little more about Mary, the Lady of the Rosary. Perhaps you're wondering why. Why does it matter if Mary is misunderstood? What does that have to do with the Rosary? With this book?

---

[9] *Roy Abraham Varghese, God Sent: A History of the Accredited Apparitions of Mary (New York, New York: The Crossroad Publishing Company 2000), p. 4.*
[10] *Ibid. p. 1.*

Well, the Rosary is a gift given to us from Her. And sometimes it is hard to love a gift you receive from someone you don't particularly like, or someone you don't really understand. How can you appreciate the gift if you misunderstand the giver, or misunderstand the motive behind the gesture?

Quite frankly, friends, if you can't appreciate Mary, you can't fully appreciate the Rosary. So, let's take a closer look, starting at the beginning.

St. Dominic, The First Preacher of the Rosary

While the Psalter of Mary (the Rosary), began early on as a substitute for the Psalter of David, it didn't gain widespread popularity and approval until much later.

In the early 1200s, there was a group known as the Albigensians who were wreaking havoc on the Church. The Albigensians believed there was no Heaven, no Hell, and no moral law. They applauded adultery, fornication, and suicide. And they did not believe in Baptism, the Eucharist, or the Incarnation of Jesus. Essentially, they believed there was a good god, but that everything in the physical world—all creation—was evil. So, there could not be a Son of God in human form.

The Albigensian heresy was spreading like wildfire and taking over southern France. St. Dominic (a priest in that area) was very disheartened by what was happening, and tried to preach against it. But had little success.

One day in the year 1208, while at his wits end in the church of Prouille, St. Dominic prayed to the Blessed

57

Virgin Mary. He complained to Her about the Albigensians, and how his preaching against their heresy had been ineffective. Mary replied to him in a vision, "Wonder not that you have obtained so little fruit by your labors. You have spent them on barren soil, not yet watered with the dew of Divine grace. When God willed to renew the face of the earth, He began by sending down on it the fertilizing rain of the Angelic Salutation. Therefore, preach my Psalter...and you will obtain an abundant harvest."

From that point on St. Dominic began to preach the Rosary. He went into the towns of heretics and taught them the Hail Mary, the Our Father, and the mysteries of the faith. He was very successful in this endeavor, which brought about a miraculous conversion of the Albigensian people.

The Rosary was so effective and so transforming for that area, that when St. Dominic heard confessions, he rarely gave a penance that was not the Rosary. And ten years later, St. Dominic started the Confraternity of the Rosary—a group of laypeople who faithfully pray all the decades of the Rosary throughout the course of each week.

This Confraternity earned approval by many Popes, such as Pope Clement VIII and Pope Alexander VI. Then, in 1679, Pope Innocent XI even confirmed multiple indulgences granted to the Confraternity:

1. Members may gain a plenary indulgence on the day of joining the Confraternity
2. A plenary indulgence at the hour of death

3. For each rosary of five decades recited, ten years and ten quarantines
4. Each time that members say the holy names of Jesus and Mary devoutly: seven days' indulgence
5. For those who assist with devotion at the procession of the holy Rosary: seven years and sever quarantines of indulgence
6. Members who have made a good confession and are genuinely sorry for their sins may gain a plenary indulgence on certain days by visiting the Rosary chapel in the church where the Confraternity is established
7. To those who assist at the Salve Regina: a hundred days' indulgence
8. To those who openly wear the rosary out of devotion and to set a good example: a hundred days indulgence
9. Sick members who are unable to church may gain a plenary indulgence by going to confession and Communion and by saying that day the whole Rosary, or at least five decades
10. The Sovereign Pontiffs have shown their generosity towards members of the Rosary Confraternity by allowing them to gain the indulgences attached to the Stations of the Cross by visiting five altars in the church where the Rosary Confraternity is established, and by saying the Our Father and Hail Mary five times before each altar, for the well-being of the Church. If there are only one or two altars in the Confraternity church, they should say the Our

Father and Hail Mary twenty-five times before one of them.[11]

Even to this day, the Catholic Church considers the Dominicans (those who followed St. Dominic) as the official promoters of both the Rosary and the Rosary Confraternity.

The Lady of the Rosary

In the first three chapters of this book, we clarified the misunderstanding that the Rosary is somehow idolatrous. It is not. But what about the misunderstanding regarding Mary? Some people still hold the notion that through Her supposed apparitions She somehow calls attention to Herself. But this is not true. If we look at the story of Her appearance to St. Dominic, we see that the apparition had nothing to do with Her. It had to do with the tragedy of the time and the loss of faith that threatened the Church.

The Blessed Virgin Mary appeared to St. Dominic because he needed Her. He called out to Her. And like a good Mother, She encouraged Him. She gave him the remedy. A remedy that brought whole masses of people back to belief in Her Son.

She did not encourage Him to preach the Rosary so that people would worship Her. She encouraged the Rosary

---

[11] *"The Secret of The Rosary"* by Saint Louis de Montfort, 1993 TAN Books, #96

so that they would bring their minds and hearts back to God. God alone is at the center of the story.

Mary is the Lady of the Rosary, not in an idolatrous way. She is the Lady of the Rosary in a prophetic way. She is the messenger, the Mother, the Protectress of the Faith (because She is espoused to the Holy Spirit who is the Guardian of the Faith). Therefore, She has a vested interest in what happens to the Church of Her Son and to its members, who are Her children.

The Rosary was not given as some trivial devotion, but as a remedy, a weapon, a gift. This speaks of the great love that Mary has for the children of God. And it speaks of the love and gratitude that we owe Her because of it—love and gratitude that is currently being withheld by many.

If your own mother gave you a priceless Christmas gift, capable of solving all your current problems, would you speak ill of the gift? Would you accuse her of just wanting attention for herself? Would you refuse the gift and abandon your mother? Probably not. And yet, this is what is happening to our Heavenly Mother, Our Lady of the Rosary.

Her gift and Her motives have been gravely misunderstood by a multitude, and it is high time we clear up the misunderstanding—which not only hurts Her, but hurts us. This is a gift for *us*, for *our* benefit. The Lady of the Rosary is not our enemy. She is the enemy of our enemy, who comes to arm us against him. It is not in our best interest to spurn Her. And, friends, it is not a sin to love Her.

We preach time and again that we are to love all people, everywhere. We love sinners and saints, musicians, actors, family and friends. But, when it comes to loving the Mother of God we get edgy, nervous, cynical. As if somehow the Lord calls us to love our neighbor, but wants us to dishonor His Mother?

This is a scrupulosity of dangerous proportions. I will even go so far as to say it is one of the devil's greatest victories—getting us to abandon the Woman of his demise. The abandonment assaults Her and disarms us. It's an "evil genius" kind-of-plan.

Alan de la Roche, The Second Preacher of the Rosary

After St. Dominic's preaching, the Rosary and the Confraternity of the Rosary remained very popular for 100 years. After that, it lost its fame, and was nearly forgotten.

In 1349, Europe suffered a terrible plague that many called the "Black Death." It started in the east and spread throughout Italy, Germany, France, Poland, and Hungary. It is said that only one out of a hundred survived it. In three years, towns were almost completely deserted.

After this, the area suffered from the heresy of Flagellants—a group of Christians who practiced public flagellation as a penance. Pope Clement VI prohibited the practice because the masters of the group violently flogged members and discouraged the sacraments, among other things. But despite this, the movement became surprisingly popular.

Then came the great Papal Schism of 1378, where the Church split because three men simultaneously claimed to be the true pope. Clearly, the Church and all of Europe had suffered greatly around this time period. It was one thing after another for many years.

Blessed Alan de la Roche, a Dominican Father (and renowned theologian) from a monastery in Brittany in Northwest France, tried to reignite the Church through his very famous sermons. But it was not enough.

As I noted in the Introduction of this book, the Lord appeared to Alan with a stern message: "You are crucifying me...because you have all the learning and understanding that you need to preach my Mother's Rosary, and you are not doing it. If you only did that, you could teach many souls the right path and lead them away from sin. But you are not doing it, and so you yourself are guilty of the sins they commit."[12]

So that he did not doubt the importance of his call, the Blessed Virgin Mary later appeared to Alan, too, imploring him to preach her Rosary:

"You were a great sinner in your youth," she said, "but I obtained the grace of your conversion from my Son. Had such a thing been possible I would have liked to have gone through all kinds of suffering to save you

---

[12] *"The Secret of The Rosary"* by Saint Louis de Montfort, 1993 TAN Books, #19

because converted sinners are a glory to me. And I would have done this also to make you worthy of preaching the rosary far and wide."[13]

To encourage him still further, St. Dominic appeared to Blessed Alan, saying, "See the wonderful results I have had through preaching the holy rosary! You and all those who love Our Lady ought to do the same so that, by means of this holy practice of the rosary, you may draw all people to the real science of the virtues."[14]

After these visions, Blessed Alan successfully preached the Rosary almost unceasingly. He is the one credited today with restoring the Rosary and the Rosary Confraternity to its former vitality after it fell by the wayside. Through his preaching, people far and wide rediscovered this devotion and were reignited in their faith.

---

[13] Ibid, #20
[14] Ibid

CHAPTER FIVE:

Stewards, Saints and Students

From the time Blessed Alan de la Roche restored the
Rosary in the 1400s, there have been many others who
have felt the call to safeguard it from extinction, to keep
the fervor going. Our Lady of the Rosary (and Her
Spouse, the Holy Spirit) encouraged countless men and
women to pray, preach, and teach the importance of
this great devotion. It is impossible to cover all of them
in this chapter, but I will list four of my favorites, who
have been very influential.

St. Louis de Montfort (1673-1716)

Born and ordained in Montfort, France, St. Louis is
known as one of the great "Marian saints" of all time.
He founded the Missionaries of the Company of Mary,
as well as other schools for poor boys and girls, and is
famous for fostering devotion to the Blessed Virgin
Mary and teaching the practice of the Rosary.

His most popular book, *True Devotion to Mary*
encourages and teaches personal consecration to Jesus
through Mary. This was especially beloved by St. John
Paul II, who claimed that reading *True Devotion*
changed his life.

Another of his books, *The Secret of the Rosary*, was also
beloved by St. John Paul II. In it, St. Louis taught the

importance of the Rosary, the power of it, and he encouraged all to pray it. I have already cited his work several times in this book. It's highly recommended read.

St. Louis de Montfort's devotion to the Rosary is also evident in the fact that he includes the Rosary as an important part of the 33-day consecration.

St. Padre Pio (1887-1968)

St. Padre Pio had a love for the Virgin Mary from the time he was a young child, when he went to the church in Pietrelcina to greet and to pray to our Lady of Graces.

When he was ordained a priest, he kept a picture of Her hanging on the wall of his cell. He glanced at Her constantly: before eating, going to sleep, every time he returned to his cell after hearing confessions. He even looked upon Her before closing his eyes at his death.

He was also known as "the Friar of the Rosary." Witnesses say he always carried it in his hand or on his arm as if it were a bracelet or a shield. He had other rosaries under his bed pillow, and on the dresser in his cell. He called the rosary his weapon.

Fr. Onorato of San Giovanni Rotondo said that one night when St. Padre Pio was sick in bed, he was unable to find his rosary beads. He yelled to Fr. Onorato, saying, "Young man, get me my weapon; give me my weapon!"

This is significant because it is a well-known fact that, while St. Pio saw many visions in his life (even from childhood), many of them were demonic. Demons tormented him in horrible forms. They sometimes scourged him with heavy chains, leaving him bruised and bleeding. Sometimes they appeared as gruesome animals.

But, with his weapon, St. Pio prayed multiple Rosaries a day—as many as sixteen some days. He said, "Love the Madonna and pray the Rosary, for her Rosary is the weapon." He said the Rosary is the weapon of defense and salvation, the weapon against the evils of the world today, and the weapon given us by Mary to use against the tricks of the infernal enemy. He said, "Satan always tries to destroy the Rosary, but he will never succeed... it triumphs on everything and everybody."

Knowing firsthand the efficacy of the Rosary, St. Padre Pio never ceased stressing its importance.

St. Maximillian Kolbe (1894-1941)

St. Maximilian Kolbe, a polish Franciscan friar, was also a great Marian priest. He was a mischievous child with a love of soldiers and all things military. When he was 12 years old, feeling unsure of his future, he asked the Virgin Mary what would become of him. She appeared to him holding two crowns—one white, the other red. She asked him if he was willing to accept either of these crowns. The white one meant that he would persevere in purity, and the red that he would become a martyr. St. Maximilian told Her that he would accept them both.

This profoundly influenced his life and his ministry in spreading devotion the Virgin Mary. He became a Catholic priest, and started a religious house with more than 800 friars, which was the largest in the world at the time. He founded the daily newspaper called the Militia Immaculata (Army of the Immaculate One), and started a monthly magazine called, "Rycerz Niepokalanej" (Knight of the Immaculate) which had over a million readers.

The military lover turned priest devoted his life to spiritual warfare, calling the Rosary the spiritual weapon of our time. He taught the importance of it and wrote meditations. He was considered the "Master of New Media" because he used all new and available forms of communication to preach and evangelize, especially when it came to Mary and the Rosary. He used emerging printing technologies for his publications, delivered them to remote areas via airplanes, started a radio station... and rumor had it he planned to start a movie studio.

His plans were interrupted though when, during World War II, he was arrested by the German Gestapo, taken to the Pawiak prison, and then transferred to Auschwitz. He suffered terrible violence and harassment during this time, but never abandoned his faith or his priesthood. After two months in Auschwitz, the guards chose various men to be starved to death, to warn others from escaping. St. Maximilian was not chosen but he volunteered to take the place of a man who had a family.

While in the starvation bunker ("Block 13"), he led the men in prayer, sought the intercession of the Virgin Mary, and remained calm. After two weeks without food or water, he was the last of the men to be found alive, and so the guards gave him a lethal injection of carbolic acid.

The Children of Fatima

From May 13th to October 13th, 1917 the Blessed Virgin Mary appeared six times to three shepherd children living in Fatima, Portugal. She appeared hovering over a holm oak tree in a cove called the Cova da Iria on the children's parents' property. She told them She was "Our Lady of the Rosary," and asked them to pray the Rosary every day. She taught them a new prayer that was to be recited in the Rosary after the Gloria at the end of each decade.

The prayer, which today is known as the "Fatima Prayer," goes like this: *"Oh, my Jesus, forgive us our sins. Save us from the fires of Hell. Lead all souls to Heaven, especially those who are in most need of Thy mercy."*

The children—Lucia, Jacinta, and Francisco—were cousins. Lucia was the oldest, at ten years old. Francisco was nine, and his sister, Jacinta, was seven. The children were born into very faith-filled families and they were taught to pray the Rosary very early on.

However, prior to the apparitions, the children would hurry through the Rosary so that they could finish quickly and then play in the fields. They developed a strategy where they would only say the word, "Hail Mary" fifty times instead of saying the entire Hail Mary prayer.

But, when the apparitions began, they were filled with deep reverence for the Rosary. They were obedient to Mary's requests, and began to pray the entire Rosary every single day. What's more, they began to teach and encourage others to do it also.

When the news broke out that the children were seeing visions, many people came to ask them questions about what they saw or ask them to ask the Lady to grant them some special favor. Some people came just to follow the children to the cove to try to see something themselves. The children often encouraged these people to pray the Rosary with them. Many times, those who did so were affected greatly—either interiorly through conviction, or exteriorly through an answered prayer or a miracle.

The children never stopped praying and preaching the Rosary. Even when they were imprisoned (because the local authorities did not believe in the apparitions), the children prayed the Rosary with the other prisoners in jail. Little Jacinta took off a medal she was wearing around her neck and asked a prisoner to hang it up for her on a nail on the wall. The children knelt before the medal. They encouraged the prisoners to do the same, and they all prayed the Rosary together.[15]

Their following was so large that on October 13th, 1917—the day of the last formal apparition—a crowd of 70,000 people joined them in the cove, where they all witnessed the miracle of the sun as it danced in the sky.

Their lives were impactful for so many, even though they were short. Francisco died of the Spanish flu just two years after the apparitions, at age eleven. Jacinta died a year later at age 10. Lucia, however, lived quite some time longer and died in 2005 at the age of 97. Francisco and Jacinta were canonized saints by Pope John Paul II in the year 2000.

St. John Paul II (1920-2005)

Born in Poland, St. John Paul II experienced great loss early in life. He lost his mother at the age of 9 and his brother at 12. Because of this, he had a great devotion to the Blessed Mother, Mary—which he kept after he was ordained a priest in 1946 and also after becoming Pope in 1978. In fact he dedicated his papacy to Her, claiming his apostolic motto was: "Totus Tuus," meaning "totally thine."

In 1987, he wrote *Redemptoris Mater* (Mother of the Redeemer), a Mariological encyclical on the Blessed

---

[15] *"Fatima in Lucia's Own Words: The Memoirs of Sister Lucia, the Last Fatima Visionary,"* Annotated by Keeping it Catholic 2015

Virgin Mary in the life of the Pilgrim Church. From 1995-1997, he gave 70 catecheses on the Blessed Virgin Mary at the Wednesday General Audiences. And in 2002, he wrote *Rosarium Virginis Mariae* (Rosary of the Virgin Mary), an Apostolic Letter declaring 2002 to 2003 the "Year of the Rosary." In this letter, he also introduced a new set of Rosary mysteries called the "Luminous Mysteries," or the "Mysteries of Light."

Students of the Rosary

Over the years, we have been blessed by so many stewards and saints. They have acceded the call to proclaim the Rosary so that it would not lose its fervor and could be handed on to us.

But, now it is *our* turn to answer the call. We are the students of the Rosary. The fact that you have opened this book confirms it. But to merely read of the Rosary is not enough. Like a college student who has read the material and must then leave the classroom to practice what he has learned in the field, so too, must we put down this text book, pick up the beads of the Rosary, and begin to practice this devotion.

We are students of the Rosary, but more precisely, we are students of Jesus, the teacher. We are students of Mary, His aid. We are students who study the model of God in the mysteries; students who proclaim the words of the Our Father which the Son taught us; students who recite the Angelic Salutation which brought Him to us.

We are students, "stewards in training," studying to become great saints. To do that we must not only understand the Rosary, we must actually pray it. This book is not just a study. It is a call.

CHAPTER SIX:

For Salvation and Peace

In the last chapter, I said that this was your "call" to pray the Rosary. Now, perhaps you are still wondering what the big deal is. Perhaps you are thinking, *"yes it sounds like a great prayer, but it is not a necessary one."*

Well... I am actually going to disagree with you and say that it absolutely _is_ necessary.

No, the Rosary is not a formal, mandatory practice or tenet of the faith. You are right. The authorities of the Church have not said that you *must* pray the Rosary. But... for approximately 600 years, both Jesus and Mary have begged us to pray it. They have appeared and spoke and tugged on the heart strings of the faithful all over the globe. The Son of God and the Mother of God are pleading for us to pray it. Doesn't that alone make it sort of a personal necessity, even if it is not a Church necessity?

Not only that, Jesus and Mary promised some amazing things to those who adhere to their requests. In fact, the Virgin Mary made fifteen promises to St. Dominic and Blessed Alan de la Roche regarding those who pray the Rosary. Here they are in Her own words:

1. To all those who shall recite my Rosary devoutly, I promise my special protection and very great graces.

2. Those who shall persevere in the recitation of my Rosary shall receive some signal grace.

3. The Rosary shall be a very powerful armor against hell; it will destroy vice, deliver from sin, and dispel heresy.

4. The Rosary will make virtue and good works flourish and will obtain for souls the most abundant divine mercies; it will substitute in hearts love of God for love of the world, and will lift them to the desire of heavenly and eternal things. How many souls shall sanctify themselves by this means!

5. Those who trust themselves to me through the Rosary, shall not perish.

6. Those who shall recite my Rosary devoutly, meditating on its mysteries, shall not be overwhelmed by misfortune. The sinner shall be converted; the just shall grow in grace and become worthy of eternal life.

7. Those truly devoted to my Rosary shall not die without the Sacraments of the Church.

8. Those who recite my Rosary shall find during their life and at their death the light of God, the fullness of His graces, and shall share in the merits of the blessed.

9. I shall deliver very promptly from purgatory the souls devoted to my Rosary.

10. The true children of my Rosary shall enjoy great glory in heaven.

11. What you ask through my Rosary, you shall obtain.

12. Those who propagate my Rosary shall be aided by me in all their necessities.
13. I have obtained from my Son that all the members of the Rosary Confraternity shall have for their brethren the saints of heaven during their life and at the hour of death.
14. Those who recite my Rosary faithfully are all my beloved children, the brothers and sisters of Jesus Christ
15. Devotion to my Rosary is a great sign of predestination.

From these promises, and the graces I have already explained in Part 1 of this book, we can see that the Rosary is a powerful way to attain personal sanctification...and to secure a place in Heaven. This is assuming, of course, that it is prayed *sincerely* from the heart with the intention of becoming holy and appeasing the Hearts of Jesus and Mary.

A Rosary that is not prayed, but merely "said" to test the promises, does not merit the rewards. Remember from chapter one that prayer requires faith, or at least the sincere desire to have faith. When we pray, God first sees our motives, then He feels our heart (our faith and love), then He hears our words.

I envision these three as the portal connecting us to God. Our motives are like the doorway out of the world. Our heart is like the hallway to God (a big heart is a short hallway, and a small heart is a long hallway). Our words are like the knock on the doorway on the other side. God cannot resist the words of His Son in the Our Father, or the words of His messenger in the Angelic Salutation. He cannot resist the echo of Mary His Mother who prays with us, and so, this opens for us the door into the Heavenly realm.

That being said, if our motives or our hearts are *not* pure, I think in some way we remain closed off... at the other end of the hall, still a long way from God. Likewise, if we are living in mortal sin. But, that is NOT to say those in mortal sin should not bother to pray, or that God is not interested in their prayer. No, Jesus listens intently for the sounds of a sinner praying. It is music to His ears. He attends to it like a lost sheep. He does everything in His power during that prayer to bring him back into the fold.

So, as long as our motives are pure—as long as we have the sincere desire to give up sin and are praying with good intention—the Blessed Virgin Mary will meet us in our prayer, and provide the grace needed to make it a fruitful prayer. Remember, She prays with us and Her echo knows no distance from God.

Because of all this—the outstanding graces and promises attached to the Rosary—it is strongly advisable for parents to teach the Rosary to their children (at the youngest ages) and to pray it with them as a family. In a world that is constantly trying to rob children of innocence, virtue, and peace—a world that is constantly trying to discredit and dismantle the faith of Jesus Christ—the grace of the Rosary will help protect them. Later in this book I give advice on how to start a Rosary prayer group in the family and in communities.

The Rosary for World Peace

The Rosary is not meant solely for personal sanctification. It's meant also for the sanctification of the world. Through mass conversions (brought about by the recitation of the Rosary), the world at large can be transformed and brought back to God.

The Virgin Mary spoke of this one hundred years ago, during World War I, when She appeared to the three shepherd children in Fatima, Portugal. On May 13, 1917, Mary told them, "Pray the Rosary every day, in order to obtain peace for the world, and the end of the war." [16]

Then, on July 13, 1917, Lucia asked the Virgin Mary, "What do you want of me?"

At this point the children did not yet know who Mary was. They knew only that She was a Lady from Heaven. In response to Lucia's question, Mary reiterated Her first request, "I want you to come here on the 13th of next month, to continue to pray the Rosary every day in honor of Our Lady of the Rosary, in order to obtain peace for the world and the end of the war, because only She can help you."

---

[16] *"Fatima in Lucia's Own Words: The Memoirs of Sister Lucia, the Last Fatima Visionary,"* Annotated by Keeping it Catholic 2015

The children were then shown a terrifying vision of Hell. They could see the souls of the damned who were blackened, shrieking, and floating in flames. They could also see various demons resembling unknown animals, black and transparent like burning coals.

The Virgin Mary then told them, "You have seen Hell where the souls of poor sinners go. To save them, God wishes to establish in the world devotion to My Immaculate Heart. If what I say to you is done, many souls will be saved and there will be peace. The war is going to end; but if people do not cease offending God, a worse one will break out during the reign of Pius XI. When you see a night illumined by an unknown light, know that this is the great sign given you by God that He is about to punish the world for its crimes, by means of war, famine, and persecutions of the Church and of the Holy Father."[17]

The Virgin Mary also asked that Russia be consecrated to Her, and that people around the world adopt what's called the First Saturday devotion. To complete the first Saturday devotion, one must go to confession, receive Holy Communion, and pray the Rosary on the first Saturday of every month for five consecutive months.

She said that if Her requests are heeded, "Russia will be converted, and there will be peace; if not, [Russia] will spread her errors throughout the world, causing wars and persecutions of the Church. The good will be martyred, the Holy Father will have much to suffer,

---

[17] Ibid

various nations will be annihilated. In the end, My Immaculate Heart will triumph. The Holy Father will consecrate Russia to Me, and she will be converted, and an era of peace will be granted to the world."

Unfortunately, Her initial requests were not heeded—the Rosary was not prayed by the majority, Russia was not consecrated to Her, and the First Saturday devotion never became mainstream—and consequently, things happened just as She said they would.

World War I came to an end, but after the aurora borealis (the Northern Lights) of 1938, World War II began. Russia proceeded to spread the errors of communism and materialism throughout the world, which threatened capitalist countries everywhere and led to the Cold War. And persecutions of the Church increased with each passing year.

Today, global persecution of Christians is growing worse than ever [18] and reports show "Christians are facing the worst persecution in history."[19] This is because it is not just violent, physical persecution that we experience (though sadly, that *is* taking place in _many_ areas). But issues near and dear to God's Heart—such as marriage, family, gender, and life—have been gravely perverted and redefined. And the faithful who support God's original design for these are openly mistreated, even within the Church itself.

---

[18] *National Catholic Reporter April 25, 2017*
[19] *Catholic Herald October 12, 2017*

The Three Eras

Much of what the Virgin Mary has predicted at Fatima has come true. Though much still remains to be seen also.

It is my personal opinion that the Virgin Mary's warning to the children referred to three different eras. If you look closely, She first said that if Russia is not converted, "she will spread her errors throughout the world, causing wars and persecutions of the Church." We have already experienced this (and are experiencing it now), as I just noted.

Next, She said, "The good will be martyred, the Holy Father will have much to suffer, various nations will be annihilated." I do not believe we have fully experienced this yet. I believe we are on the precipice... on the threshold, ready to take the plunge any day.

The world right now is simmering in animosity—animosity between countries and people. We are nearing the full-boil of World War III and the "annihilation of nations." We are approaching the fulfillment of the second part of Her warning and we literally have the solution to prevent it at our fingertips (the Rosary). We have the remedy of all remedies that can save the world from utter destruction, but most people reject it.

What will it take for us to take this seriously?

Friends, if we do not learn from history (from what occurred after the message of Fatima), then we are doomed to repeat it. If we do not return to God, He will do as the Virgin said: punish the world for its crimes, by means of war, famine, and more persecutions. This time it will be greater than ever before because our sins and our reluctance is greater than ever before.

But it doesn't have to be that way. All we need to do is pick up a Rosary. All we need to do is pray that the Pope finally consecrates Russia to the Immaculate Heart of Mary, that the simmering animosity between nations cools, and the world finally returns to God.

So, is the Rosary a mandatory tenet of the faith? No. But it *is* necessary because you, friend, have a part to play in this unfolding story of the salvation of the world. It is to pray the Rosary for world peace, and perhaps begin the First Saturday devotion too.

If you feel led, you can also formally petition the cause for the consecration of Russia. Vatican Cardinal Raymond Burke has called on the Catholic faithful to "work for the consecration of Russia to the Immaculate Heart of Mary" in fidelity to the request by Our Lady of Fatima. There is an online petition you can sign at the following address: https://lifepetitions.com/petition/consecrate-russia-to-the-immaculate-heart-of-mary-petition

CHAPTER SEVEN:

For Atonement and Life

Each time the Virgin Mary appeared to the three children in Fatima, she told them to pray the Rosary. This was the common thread weaving through all the messages. In addition to that, She asked them to make reparation—to make amends or restitution for the sins that have been committed—so as to appease the Heart God and avert His justice. She also asked the children to make sacrifices for sinners.

As I already noted, the Rosary is a very deep, powerful and effective prayer. But it is also a sacrificial prayer because of the time it takes to pray it and the distractions we must fight against to persevere in it. When the sacrifice of the Rosary is offered to God on behalf of someone else—especially sinners—our love of neighbor makes it particularly effective. (Remember the hallway of your heart?) It's not *just* the Rosary, though. We can offer God any sacrifice, difficulty or trial.

The Virgin Mary explained to the children, "Sacrifice yourself for sinners, and say many times, especially whenever you make some sacrifice, 'O Jesus it is for love of Thee, for the conversion of sinners, and in reparation for the sins against the Immaculate Heart of Mary.'"[20]

---

[20] *"Fatima in Lucia's Own Words: The Memoirs of Sister Lucia, the Last Fatima Visionary,"* Annotated by Keeping it Catholic 2015

Now, perhaps you're wondering: what are the sins against the Immaculate Heart of Mary? And why make reparation for those?

I know, some people get uncomfortable with this. They think it is blasphemous to talk about sins against Mary because technically we can only sin against God. Yes, this is true. People sin against God. But quite often, people sin against God *because* they offend His Mother, Mary.

Let's face it. You don't mess with someone's mother. That's just a common, well-known fact. It's the mentality behind the old, "your momma" fight strategy. The idea is that when you really want to get at someone, when you want to really attack them, upset them, or hurt them... you insult their mom. Because somehow in the depths of the human heart, mothers are sacred and off limits.

Except when it comes to Mary. For some reason, the Mother of God is offended on a regular basis, even by Christians who profess to love Her Son. But we need to understand that this hurts Jesus. This offends Him. This is a sin against Him, via Her.

In 1930, Jesus appeared to Lucia of Fatima (who, by this time, was a religious sister living in Spain). He told her there are five ways in which people offend and blaspheme against His Mother. They are:

1. The blasphemies against the Immaculate Conception
2. The blasphemies against her virginity

3. The blasphemies against the Divine Maternity, refusing at the same time to accept her as the Mother of all mankind
4. The blasphemies of those who try publicly to implant in the children's hearts indifference contempt, and even hatred against this Immaculate Mother
5. The blasphemies of those who insult her directly in her sacred images.[21]

These are hurtful on multiple levels. One, they directly hurt the Virgin Mary because they are directed at Her. Two, they directly hurt God because She is His Mother. Three, they hurt us because She has been chosen to be our Mother and our Protectress. Four, they hurt the world because the peace of the world has been entrusted to Her.

In addition, it is my personal belief that there are indirect sins that seriously offend the Virgin Mary also. Because of Her chastity, charity, purity, modesty, and sublimity, the Virgin Mary is the model of *all* virtues. It's just who She is. Since She is also our Mother (and Her job is to instill these virtues in us), it hurts Her terribly when we sin against these virtues—when we sin against modesty, purity, or any of the others.

Think of a mother with strong beliefs, who tries to raise a child in her beliefs. Let's say one day the mother discovers the child has gone against her teaching, and in doing so, has injured himself, almost fatally. The mother

---

[21] *"Lucia Speaks, Memoirs and Letters of Sister Lucia"* (Wash., NJ: AMI Press, 1976), p. 238.

feels the heartache caused by infidelity to the beliefs that she has taught, as well as the heartache of watching the child self-destruct. It's a double agony.

This is how we hurt the Virgin Mary when we sin against the virtues that She embodies. Not only have we been unfaithful to Her teaching—not only have we gone against everything She stands for and everything She is—but sinning against certain virtues can be near fatal for us. They can injure our relationship with God and rob us of grace. So, She suffers again, watching us self-destruct. It's a double agony.

And yes, we *are* self-destructing. On a global scale, we are abandoning the commandments of God, forsaking all that He holds dear, and adopting that which He has plainly said He detests. Nothing is sacred anymore. Nothing. Not even the most basic of things—faith, marriage, gender, sex. Every single principle of God has been twisted and perverted to the most heinous degree. Nothing is left untouched.

This, my friends, requires _serious_ atonement. And what better atonement can we offer God, than the Rosary?

The Rosary makes atonement for the sins committed against Mary (because it's Her Rosary and She prays with us), but it also makes atonement for the sins committed against God, (because the central focus of the Rosary is Jesus). So, it's a double atonement, if you will.

This is why the Rosary was included in the First Saturday devotion that was mentioned in the last chapter.

Because the purpose of this devotion is specifically to make reparation for the sins committed against the Immaculate Heart of Mary (this must be our intention when completing First Saturdays)... and Jesus has attached a great deal of significance to it.

On March 19, 1939, Lucia wrote, "Whether the world has war or peace depends on the practice of this devotion, along with the consecration to the Immaculate Heart of Mary."

Whether the world has war or peace? Well clearly, today, we do _not_ have peace. The world faces the imminent risk of a nuclear world war, and is utterly besieged by terrorism. The threats are real and looming and grave. But... we have a way to combat all this.

The army of Mary must pick up the weapon of the Rosary and fight on our knees—destroying the strongholds of the enemy, appeasing the King's heart, and defending the honor of the Queen. At this point, there is no other way. We have lost too much ground already.

So, we must fight—not against people, not "against flesh and blood, but against principalities, against powers, against the rulers of the darkness of this age." (Eph. 6:12) We are fighting evil. _Unseen_ powers and principalities and rulers. The Kingdom of God is battling the Kingdom of Satan. The Rosary is _the_ weapon of choice, designed specifically for these most dire times.

The Battle For Life

In every war, there are the major, decisive battles that either cause you to win the war, or lose it. It is no different in this spiritual war. The most decisive battle we experience currently is not against terrorism or maniacs testing nuclear arms. It is against abortion.

According to the World Health Organization, there are approximately 125,000 abortions occurring each day around the world, which corresponds to 40-50 million abortions every year. That's 40-50 million distinct, eternal souls created by God, loved intensely, blessed with innate purpose. Just wiped off the planet.

That's millions of family trees snuffed out in an instant. Millions of vocations—millions of parents, priests, ministers—millions of chosen personalities gifted with the ability to change the world for the better. Millions of gifts, crafted lovingly by the Hand of God, given to us for our benefit. Now gone. All gone. Many even thrown in dumpsters.

Do not be deceived. Do not think this is just some political issue, like taxes or jobs. This, my friends, is the battle of all battles, the battle that will inevitably decide our fate.

This is a sin of astronomical proportions. It is a direct sin against the very essence of God, because it is a sin against life itself which comes from God. It is a sin against His generosity, His will, His plan. It is a sin against the incarnation of Jesus who made pregnancy sacred when He chose it as the means by which to come and save the world. It is a sin against the Holy Spirit who breathes life into each soul that takes residence in a womb. It is a sin against Mary who, even though Her pregnancy was unplanned, chose life for _our_ sake.

This. Is. THE. Battle. And the Virgin Mary has come to warn us.

On July 13, 1997—exactly 80 years (to the day) after the Virgin Mary asked the children of Fatima to pray the Rosary for peace and atonement—Mary appeared to another visionary, this time in America.

Maureen Sweeny-Kyle was praying in a church in Ohio, when suddenly Mary appeared in the Church, holding a large beaded Rosary. The 50 Hail Mary beads changed into the shapes of the 50 states and then slipped off the string of the Rosary and landed in a pile at Mary's feet.

A few days later on July 17th, She appeared to Maureen again with all 50 states still in a pile at Her feet. There were two angels with Her this time. One angel picked up one of the states and handed it to the other angel. It was like sand in his hand. Then it turned into gold with some of the sand falling out as it changed. The gold was then given to the Virgin Mary who placed it into Her Immaculate Heart.

The Virgin Mary said to Maureen: "These are the faithful and righteous who have persevered in faith... Humbly understand that you are living in apocalyptic times and that this is a place of revelation—holy revelation. Tonight, I am asking you to accept your place in these times and to increase the grace in your hearts by your efforts through prayer and sacrifice."

This message echoed the message She gave the children at Fatima 80 years prior.

Almost a month later, on August 10th 1997, the Virgin Mary appeared to Maureen once again. This time all 50 states were in a pile at Her feet and they are smoldering as if they were ashes. She gave Maureen a message that was to be made public for all people.

She said, "Abortion is the evil which races your country towards destruction. Only if this evil is overturned in hearts and in the world, can your nation be saved from certain death. Dear children, the tribulations have begun and proceed as labor pains of a woman with child, each one stronger and more telling than the one before. I come to you asking you to stop the death and destruction and the loss of life and souls... Dear children, you are the solution and the victory; therefore, pray, pray, pray."

Once again, just as She had done so many times before with so many different seers, the Virgin Mary came to warn us of coming chastisements, and to plead with us to pray the Rosary.

She then appeared to Maureen with a different kind of Rosary. Instead of the 50 states, the beads on this Rosary were shaped like blue tear drops. Inside the 50 tear drops were 50 tiny fetuses curled up like they would be in a womb. The Virgin Mary called this the "Rosary of the Unborn" and asked Maureen to have it made for the public. It was a long, difficult task finding someone who could mass produce such a detailed bead... but five years later, the task was completed.

After it was completed, Mary and Jesus appeared to Maureen with special promises to those who pray the Rosary of the Unborn. The Virgin Mary said, "I affirm to you, my daughter, that each Hail Mary prayed from a loving heart will rescue one of these innocent lives from death by abortion." (July 2, 2001)

That means 50 Hail Marys prayed on the Rosary of the Unborn will save 50 babies from abortion! Think how many babies that saves each week, each month, each year if we pray it daily! And that's not all it does.

A month later Jesus appeared to Maureen and said: "Every rosary prayed from the heart to its completion on these beads mitigates the punishment as yet withstanding for the sin of abortion...When I say 'punishment as yet withstanding'...I mean the punishment each soul deserves for taking part in this sin. Then too, I also refer to the greater punishment that awaits the world for embracing this sin." (August 3, 2001)

On August 13, 2006, Jesus appeared again and said, "Today, my brothers and sisters, you fear—and with good cause—the event of a nuclear war...because of nuclear fallout...and yet I tell you, that the fallout from praying the Rosary of the Unborn is much more powerful than any nuclear bomb. You will not have an end to these threats against world peace until abortion is eliminated."

The "Secret" Weapon

It was ironic that Jesus gave the above message to Maureen on the 13th of the month, since it was on the 13th of the each month that Mary appeared to the children in Fatima. It is also ironic that He spoke of nuclear war, because it eerily resembles something else the children of Fatima were shown during that July 13th apparition.

They were shown what is now known as the "Third Secret of Fatima." It is called this because it was the third part of the apparition, and the children were to keep it a secret. In 1944, Lucia wrote it down, put it in a sealed envelope and gave it to the then Bishop of Leiria-Fatima. Sister Lucia wrote on the outside of the envelope that it could be opened only after 1960, either by the Patriarch of Lisbon or the Bishop of Leiria. [22]

After it was opened, it was sent to the Vatican and locked it up until the year 2000. This is what the children saw, in Lucia's own words.

"...At the left of Our Lady and a little above, we saw an angel with a flaming sword in his left hand; flashing, it gave out flames that looked as though they would set the world on fire; but they died out in contact with the splendor that Our Lady radiated toward him from her right hand: pointing to the earth with his right hand, the

---

[22] *"Nine Things to Know and Share About the Third Secret of Fatima" by Jimmy Aikin, National Catholic Register May 12, 2013*

angel cried out in a loud voice: 'Penance, Penance, Penance!'

And we saw in an immense light that is God: 'something similar to how people appear in a mirror when they pass in front of it' a bishop dressed in white 'we had the impression that it was the Holy Father.'

"Other bishops, priests, men and women religious going up a steep mountain, at the top of which there was a big cross of roughhewn trunks as of a cork tree with the bark; before reaching there the Holy Father passed through a big city half in ruins and half trembling with halting step, afflicted with pain and sorrow, he prayed for the souls of the corpses he met on his way; having reached the top of the mountain, on his knees at the foot of the big cross he was killed by a group of soldiers who fired bullets and arrows at him, and in the same way there died one after another the other bishops, priests, men and women religious, and various lay people of different ranks and positions. Beneath the two arms of the cross there were two angels each with a crystal aspersorium in his hand, in which they gathered up the blood of the martyrs and with it sprinkled the souls that were making their way to God." [23]

This is full of intense imagery and mystery, but two things came to mind when I read it. The first is the mountain of God, which reminds me of the mountain

---

[23] *"Fatima in Lucia's Own Words: The Memoirs of Sister Lucia, the Last Fatima Visionary,"* Annotated by Keeping it Catholic 2015

image from my book *"Victory in the Spiritual Garden."* That mountain is a spiritual one—it symbolizes the internal spiritual journey we take out of the city of man (the world), into the city of God (Heaven). I did not think of the Third Secret when I originally wrote that book, but looking back, the similarities are uncanny.

The second thing that comes to mind is nuclear war, primarily because she described a group of soldiers (indicating war) and devastation, a city half in ruins (indicating nuclear). She also described the angel's flaming sword (in Scripture, fire often indicates God's justice). And She said it looked as though it could set the world on fire, which also alludes to nuclear.

So, when I look at this Third Secret, I see both a physical and spiritual struggle, involving an internal dying to self as well as a physical dying. Now, granted, nuclear war is my own speculation, of course... but when the Third Secret was released in 2000, Cardinal Joseph Ratzinger (who later became Pope Benedict XVI) made the same speculation when he, too, alluded to nuclear war.

He wrote, "Today the prospect that the world might be reduced to ashes by a sea of fire no longer seems pure fantasy: Man himself, with his inventions, has forged the flaming sword" [24]

Perhaps this is why the secret was not to be opened until after 1960. In 1944, when Lucia wrote it down, the threat of nuclear war would not have been understood.

---

[24] *Congregation for the Doctrine of the Faith, "The Message of Fatima"* www.vatican.va *June 26, 2000*

But after 1960, and after the Cold War, it would have been... and is now for sure. We know all too well the devastating would-be effects of a nuclear world war. And yet, somehow, we are still jaded and indifferent to Her plea.

One hundred years after warning three children in Fatima Portugal, the Blessed Virgin Mary is now warning a woman in Ohio... because, after one hundred years, we still haven't listened to Her. We still consider Her messages to be fanatical, even though news outlets confirm the possibility of nuclear war is not fanatical, but very real.

The flaming sword of justice has been raised, because we have abandoned God and His laws, blasphemed His Mother, and slaughtered billions of babies on the altar of abortion. The only thing that can stop it from striking, is grace from the Virgin Mary. As Lucia recalls, "[the flames] died out in contact with the splendor that Our Lady radiated." We receive this grace through the Rosary.

Mary confirmed this on July 19, 2016 when She appeared to Maureen, holding the same Rosary of the fifty states. She said, "Now, more than ever, is the time when I need rosaries for your country... The future of your nation depends upon it."

She returned to Maureen on August 21, 2016, and said, "These are desperate times. Many do not realize the grave urgency of prayer for this nation... Souls are at stake. Lives are at stake. Dear children, you are engaged in war - spiritual and physical war. Your weapon is this."

She holds up the Rosary of the States. Then it changes into the Rosary of the Unborn. "Pray for an end to abortion which is Satan's weapon of mass destruction."

CHAPTER EIGHT:

When the Rosary Won Wars and Saved Lives

So far in this book I have made some pretty, big claims. I've said the Rosary is the most complete prayer, the most powerful prayer, the most productive prayer. I've said it can save babies and souls and the world itself. I've said it's a weapon, and it's THE answer to ALL of life's difficulties. I know, it sounds unbelievable. At this point, maybe you're looking for proof. Maybe you're wondering, "Oh yeah? When?" When did the prayer of the Rosary ever help?"

It's an easy question to answer because the instances are numerous. The hardest part is choosing which ones to tell you about, so I don't make this section of the book too long. I want to include these in this book, though, in the hopes that they will fan the flames of your faith so that you believe in the power of this devotion. Remember how important faith is when we pray. May the stories in these next two chapters encourage you, and give you hope.

Now, let's start with instances when the Rosary won wars and saved lives. Though let me be clear, it is not the string of beads itself that has done this, as if it is some superstition. No, it is God through the Virgin Mary who has won wars and saved lives. He did it in response to His people praying the Rosary, though.

Lepanto

In the year 622, Mohammed attempted to conquer the entire Christian world for Allah by force. Within a hundred years, his people had taken over and robbed every Christian capital of the Middle East, from Antioch through North Africa and Spain. The only thing he had not taken was the northern area from Southern France to Constantinople.

For hundreds of years battles continued, and the Turks expanded their empire in all four directions. Everywhere they went they set huge fires of destruction, desecrated Christian churches, and tortured and murdered the people.

By 1540, it grew even worse. Because of the Protestant Reformation, the Church split, and no longer fought as one, so Christians were easier prey. Muslims then threatened to attack Venice and Rome, which could have been the collapse of Christian Europe. Pope St. Pius V recognized the danger of this, and called on the leaders of the West to unite against them.

Finally, in September of 1571, Don Juan of Austria, (the younger brother of King Phillip II), led a makeshift fleet of Catholic ships, called the Holy League (mainly from Spain, Venice and Genoa), out against the much larger fleet of the Ottoman Empire. The Holy League was gravely outnumbered 3 to 1.

However, Pope Pius V, ordered all churches to remain open for prayer day and night. He asked the faithful to petition the intercession of the Blessed Virgin Mary by praying the Rosary. Even the men on the ships prayed the Rosary and implored Her help.

Then, on October 7, 1571, the two opposing forces met within fighting distance of each other, just south of the town of Lepanto.

The Ottoman Empire waved a green battle flag with the name of Muhommad embroidered on it in Arabic some 29,800 times. The Holy League had Rosaries, and an image of Our Lady of Guadalupe, that had been touched to the original image on Juan Diego's cloak.

The Turk ships normally approached battle in crescent formation, but as they neared the Holy League, a wind picked up that brought them into a straight line. This gave the Holy League an advantage, despite being outnumbered.

The Holy League lost 50 of its ships in the battle. The Turks lost much more—about 210 of its 250 ships—and their leader Ali Pasha was killed, along with 25,000 of his sailors. This victory at Lepanto, stopped Ottoman invasion into the Mediterranean and prevented them from spreading through Europe and overcoming the Christian West.

At the hour of victory the pope—who was hundreds of miles away at the Vatican—is said to have gotten up from a meeting, walked over to an open window exclaiming "The Christian fleet is victorious!" and shed tears of joy and thanksgiving to God.

He later formally declared that day, October 7th, the feast of Our Lady of Victory (which was later changed to the Feast of Our Lady of the Rosary).

New Orleans

In the fall of 1814, the Revolutionary War of 1812 was still underway. A British fleet of more than 50 ships led by General Edward Pakenham set out into the Gulf of Mexico to attack New Orleans and block the Mississippi River. the American troops under General Andrew Jackson prepared for battle. The Americans, though, were outnumbered 15,000 to 6,000. So, it looked like they were doomed.

The night before, however, the people of New Orleans went to a convent where the Ursuline Order of Sisters were. They prayed the Rosary through the night for the impending battle.

The next morning, Mass was offered. The Prioress at the convent vowed that if the Americans won, they would have a Mass of Thanksgiving annually. During Communion at the Mass, a messenger ran into the chapel and said the British had been defeated. They had been confused by a fog.

The annual Mass of Thanksgiving has been held ever since.

Hiroshima

On August 6, 1945, towards the end of World War II, America dropped the first atomic bomb on Hiroshima, Japan. This explosion killed 80,000 people almost immediately. Three days after Hiroshima was hit, a second bomb was dropped on Nagasaki, killing 40,000 people. Because of radiation exposure, tens of thousands of others died in the months and years following these bombings. Almost everyone was affected in some way.

That is, except for some priests living in Hiroshima.

The Jesuit priests Hugo Lassalle, Hubert Schiffer, Wilhelm Kleinsorge, and Hubert Cieslik withfour others, were at the rectory of the church of Our Lady of the Assumption, which was located near the hypocenter of the blast (basically, ground zero). Their rectory, though, remained standing while the buildings all around it were flattened immediately. In fact, an estimated 90% of people in the hypocenter died instantly. Most of the remaining people died quickly afterwards, because of the severity of the wounds they suffered.

The four Jesuits, however, had just minor injuries from broken windows. Nothing else. Doctors warned them that radiation exposure would produce serious lesions, as well as serious illnesses and early death. But it never happened. Over the next several years, they were examined by dozens of doctors approximately 200 times. There was never any trace of the radiation found in their bodies.

How could this possibly be true? In 1976, Fr Schiffer gave this testimony, "we survived because we were living the message of Fatima. We lived and prayed the rosary daily in that home."[25]

Florida

At 3: 00 am Ted Bundy broke into a sorority house at Florida State University. He killed two girls and began searching for more victims. He entered a third girl's room holding a bat. When he saw that the girl had a rosary in her hand, he dropped the bat, and ran out of the sorority house.

When the girl was questioned by authorities, she told them a story about her grandma. Before she left for college she promised her grandmother that she would pray the rosary every night for protection, even if she fell asleep while doing it. This is what she was doing when Ted Bundy broke into her dorm room.

Later, when Ted Bundy was on death row, he asked for a priest to be his spiritual counselor. The priest asked about that terrible night at Florida State University. Bundy explained that when he entered the girl's room, he fully intended to murder her, but as he said, "some mysterious power prevented me." [26]

---

[25] *The Priests Who Survived the Atomic Bomb, by Donal Anthony Foley, The Catholic Herald August 9, 2015*
[26] *"With Mary to Jesus" Fr. Joseph Esper Queenship Publishing Company (2010)*

Rwanda

During the 1994 Rwandan genocide Immaculée Ilibagiza (who was home on Easter break from the National University of Rwanda, where she had been studying to become an engineer) was hidden for 91 days with seven other Tutsi women in a small, 3x4 foot bathroom, in a pastor's home. Immaculée's father had sent her running to the pastor's house when a crowd of machete-armed Hutu invaded their family's home in Mataba. Pastor Murinzi, a Hutu, did not share in the ethnic hatred between Hutu and Tutsi that was common in Rwanda in 1994. So, he took in eight Tutsi women who begged for refuge at his home.

For over three months, the women stayed in this bathroom, which was hidden in a room behind a wardrobe. Immaculee explained, "I said 27 Rosaries every day—literally. And I counted! I had nothing else to do in that bathroom. So I said 27 Rosaries every day and 40 Divine Mercy chaplets every day. But we [in the bathroom] never spoke with each other. All we did was this [pray]. ... It helped my sanity."[27]

During the genocide, Ilibagiza's mother, father, and two brothers were killed by Hutu Interahamwe soldiers, along with more than one million others. But, after the horrific ordeal was over, Immaculée walked out of the bathroom, alive, weighing only 65 pounds.

---

[27] *"Rwandan Genocide Survivor Immaculée Ilibagiza" by Peter Jesserer Smith Nationa Catholic Register January 26, 2017*

What's even more miraculous, when she later came face-to-face with the man who macheted her mother and one of her brothers to death, she said, "I forgive you." This too, she attributes to the Rosary, which she has continued to pray every day since.

CHAPTER NINE:

When the Rosary Delivered, Healed, And Converted Souls

It is hard to relay all the different miraculous stories associated with the Rosary, but aside from winning wars and saving lives, many of them fall into the categories of deliverance, healings and conversions.

Deliverance

Blessed Alan de la Roche knew a man who tried desperately, with all kinds of different devotions to rid himself of an evil spirit that possessed him. But unfortunately, he did not have any success. Finally, he thought of wearing his Rosary around his neck, which seemed to ease his torment. He found that whenever he took it off, the devil tormented him cruelly, so he wore it night and day. Blessed Alan testified that he delivered a great number of those who were possessed by putting a Rosary around their necks. [28]

St. Louis de Montfort told of Father Jean Amet, who was in the Order of St. Dominic. Fr. Amet was giving a series of Lenten sermons in the Kingdom of Aragon one

---

[28] *"The Secret of The Rosary"* by Saint Louis de Montfort, 1993 TAN Books, #87

year, when a young girl was brought to him possessed by the devil. After he had exorcised her several times without any success, he put his Rosary around her neck. As soon as he did this, the girl began to scream and cry out terrified, "Take it off, take it off! These beads are tormenting me!" The priest had pity for the girl, and took his rosary off her.

The very next night, when Fr. Amet was in bed, the same devils who had possession of the girl came to him, foaming with rage. They tried to seize him, but he had his Rosary clasped in his hand and no efforts of theirs could wrench it from him. He beat them with it, and put them to flight, saying, "Holy Mary, Our Lady of the Rosary, come to my help!"

The next day on his way to the church, he met the poor girl, still possessed. One of the devils was with her and started to taunt him, saying, "Well, brother, if you had been without your Rosary, we should have made short shrift of you." Then Father threw his Rosary around the girl's neck and said, "By the sacred names of Jesus and Mary his holy Mother, and by the power of the holy Rosary, I command you, evil spirits, to leave the body of this girl at once." They were immediately forced to obey him, and she was delivered.

This, apparently, is not uncommon. During an exorcism the devil told Fr. Amorth (the chief exorcist for the Vatican), "Every Hail Mary of the Rosary is a blow to the head for me. If Christians knew the power of the Rosary it would be the end of me." [29]

Healing

While the stories of healing associated with the Rosary are numerous, I will relay just a few here.

In October of 1938, twenty-nine year old Patrick Peyton of County Mayo, Ireland started coughing blood. Doctors found he had advanced stages of Tuberculosis, which in those days was incurable. Patrick consecrated himself to Mary and devoted himself to praying the rosary. The patches on his lungs disappeared with no scientific explanation whatsoever. Doctors were stunned. Patrick then vowed to Mary that he would promote the rosary for his entire life, and on June 15, 1941, he was ordained a Catholic priest.

From then on Father Peyton used all forms of electronic media to preach the Rosary, specifically that families must pray the Rosary together. Father Peyton is responsible for coining the phrase, "The family that prays together, stays together." He died peacefully on June 3, 1992 with a rosary in his hands.

St. Louis de Montfort also told of the miraculous healing of Alphonsus, the King of Leon and Galicia:

---

[29] *"Devil admits to exorcist: 'I'm afraid of the Madonna'" by Gelsomino Del Guercio, Aleteia July 2, 2017*

"Alphonsus very much wanted all his servants to honor the Blessed Virgin by saying the Rosary. So, he used to hang a large rosary on his belt and always wore it, but unfortunately never said it himself. Nevertheless, his wearing it encouraged his courtiers to say the Rosary very devoutly.

One day the King fell seriously ill and when he was given up for dead he found himself, in a vision, before the judgment seat of Our Lord. Many devils were there accusing him of all the sins he had committed and Our Lord as Sovereign Judge was just about to condemn him to hell when Our Lady appeared to intercede for him. She called for a pair of scales and had his sins placed in one of the balances whereas she put the rosary that he had always worn on the other scale, together with all the Rosaries that had been said because of his example. It was found that the Rosaries weighed more than his sins.

Looking at him with great kindness Our Lady said: "As a reward for this little honor that you paid me in wearing my Rosary, I have obtained a great grace for you from my Son. Your life will be spared for a few more years. See that you spend these years wisely, and do penance."

When the King regained consciousness he cried out: "Blessed be the Rosary of the Most Holy Virgin Mary, by which I have been delivered from eternal damnation!"

After he had recovered his health he spent the rest of his life in spreading devotion to the Holy Rosary and said it faithfully every day."[30]

Fertility

While there are many stories associated with physical healings from various diseases and illnesses, there are also stories of healings from infertility. Probably one of the oldest, and more well known, is the story of the Queen of France, Blanche of Castille. The Queen was childless for the first twelve years of her marriage. She was grief stricken that she could not conceive. When St. Dominic went to see her, he advised her to pray the Rosary every day to ask God for the grace of motherhood. She did exactly as St. Dominic advised and in 1213 she gave birth to a son named Phillip. The child died in infancy, however, and so the Queen asked for help in praying for another child. She had a large number of Rosaries given out to people in the Kingdom and asked them to pray to God for a blessing. In 1215, St. Louis was born, the prince who would become the glory of France and the model of Christian Kings. [31]

Miracle of the Sun

As noted earlier, the Virgin Mary repeatedly asked the children of Fatima to pray the Rosary daily, which they did. She also told them that during the last apparition,

---

[30] *"The Secret of The Rosary"* by Saint Louis de Montfort, 1993 TAN Books, #29
[31] *Ibid #98*

She would perform a great miracle so that no one could ever doubt the apparitions took place.

On October 13, 1917 approximately 70,000 people gathered with the children to pray the Rosary, hoping to see a miracle. Even though it had been raining terribly, the sun broke through the clouds, looking like a silver sphere that spun and danced in the sky. Its rays gave off numerous, brilliant colors. Then, it seemed to thrust itself toward the crowd. People who were in attendance cried out in terror, thinking it was be the end of the world. But before sun reached earth, it returned to its place in the sky. The witnesses, who were drenched in rain, were now completely dry, and all the mud had dried up as well. During that apparition, Mary identified Herself as Our Lady of the Rosary. Many people were cured of diseases, and many others were converted to the faith.

Gold Rosaries

There is one other miraculous phenomenon that I would like to mention, one that is actually fairly common. It has been reported by many different people, all over the world, that their once-silver Rosary has miraculously changed to gold. This has happened to several people that I know personally, and I have seen their Rosaries with my own eyes.

There are numerous accounts of this taking place while visiting Marian apparition sites, but it is also occurring privately in people's homes as they pray. What could possibly be the significance of this?

It is my personal belief that these miracles are given to people to encourage them to continue praying the Rosary. I think the change in color signifies that prayer changes things, and the Rosary prayer specifically has the most dramatic affect on our lives.

To me, this is not out of character for the Blessed Virgin Mary, who has encouraged the recitation of the Rosary in nearly every corner of the globe since the time She lived on it. I hope that reading these stories will excite your heart and enliven your faith. I hope they encourage you to make this devotion a regular practice. I promise you, there is no practice as valuable as this.

CHAPTER TEN:

How to Join the Confraternity and Start a Rosary Group

As noted earlier in this book, the Rosary Confraternity is a spiritual group or association. The members are committed to praying 15 decades of the Rosary regularly. St. Louis de Montfort said there are three kinds of membership though: Ordinary Membership, which entails saying the complete Rosary of at least 15 decades once a week; Perpetual Membership, which requires it to be said only once a year; Daily Membership, which obliges one to say all 15 decades every day. None of these oblige under the pain of sin," he said. "It is not even a venial sin to fail in this duty because such an undertaking is entirely voluntary and supererogatory."[32]

Of course, people should not join the Confraternity if they do not intend to really fulfill the obligation. And they should pray it without neglecting the duties of their state in life. "Whenever the Rosary clashes with a duty of one's state in life, holy as the Rosary is, one must give preference to the duty to be performed." [33]

---

[32] *"The Secret of The Rosary"* by Saint Louis de Montfort, 1993 TAN Books, #21
[33] *Ibid*

They form a special union together with hundreds of thousands of others throughout the world, who not only pray for their own intentions, but also for the intentions and needs of all the members of the Confraternity.

Joining the Confraternity is simple. You can fill out an online form at www.Rosary-Center.org or send your written request to: The Rosary Center, PO Box 3617, Portland, OR 97208, USA. That's it. Filling out the online form takes less than five minutes and the benefits of enrolling are tremendous, as already mentioned. If you are committed to praying the Rosary, I strongly advise you to consider formally joining the Confraternity.

If you do not currently pray the Rosary, but want to start, and are concerned about finding enough time to devote to it, I suggest starting where you are comfortable and where you are able. Perhaps you think you can only say one decade at this point. That is fine. Start there.

Perhaps after you finish reading this book, you could get four or five other people together—friends, family, or co-workers—people who would also want to pray one decade each day with you. Each person can then be assigned a specific decade (the first decade or the second decade, etc.) and your group will pray a five-decade rosary every day.

Then, when each of you pray, you can offer your prayers for all of your group's intentions. That way, each of you will benefit from the entire Rosary that you all pray, collectively. Or, you can get a group of ten people who will each pray two decades, so that you pray all twenty decades together every single day.

To make it easier, you can fill out the chart at the end of this chapter and then photocopy it for the other members of your group. That way, everyone will know which mystery each group member has, so as to offer a more unified prayer.

This strategy could be especially helpful for those of you parents who have children who are in high school or college, who are not home as often as you would like. If you want to start doing a family Rosary with them, perhaps you could start out this way. If each person is assigned a decade or two every day, they could say it on their own time. Then, by the day's end, your family will have prayed an entire Rosary together. Each person can access Rosary meditations and family prayers on my website via their computer or smartphone at www.StacyMal.com.

In addition, it is also beneficial to start a physical Rosary prayer group where members meet in person. This can take place once a week or even once a month, with members praying privately outside of this meeting. It can be two people, ten people, 100 people or more.

This can be done at your parish, a school, or someone's home. If your group lives at a distance from each other, and cannot meet in person, maybe you could get together online through a video conferencing technology like Zoom, GoToMeeting, or even through Skype or Google Hangout.

Multiple people can log on at once, via their computer or smartphone. They can see each other and pray together. Perhaps one person leads each decade and the rest of the group responds. Or perhaps you have several designated leaders, one for each decade.

Regardless of how you do it, the benefits of communal prayer are numerous. St. Louis declares that, "of all the ways of saying the holy Rosary, the most glorious to God, most salutary to our souls, and the most terrible to the devil is that of saying or chanting the Rosary publicly in two choirs."[34]

Jesus Himself confirmed the power of communal prayer when He promised, "For where two or three gather in my name, there am I with them." (Mt. 18:20)

St. Louis added that praying in a group is beneficial because, "When we pray in common, the prayer of each one belongs to the whole group and make all together but one prayer, so that if one person is not praying well, someone else in the same gathering who is praying better makes up for his deficiency. In the same way, those who are strong uphold the weak, those who are fervent inspire the lukewarm, the rich enrich the poor, the bad are merged with the good...

"One who says his Rosary alone only gains the merit of one Rosary; but if he says it with thirty other people he gains the merit of thirty Rosaries. This is the law of

---

[34] *"The Secret of The Rosary"* by Saint Louis de Montfort, 1993 TAN Books, #131

public prayer. How profitable, how advantageous this is!" [35]

What's more, in 1626, in his brief Ad perpetuam rei memoriam, Pope Urban VIII attached a hundred days' extra indulgence, whenever the Rosary was said communally in two choirs.

"Finally," St. Louis said, "when the Rosary is said in common, it is far more formidable to the devil, because in this public prayer it is an army that is attacking him. He can often overcome the prayer of an individual, but if it is joined to that of others, the devil has much more trouble in getting the best of it. It is easy to break a single stick; but If you join it to others to make a bundle, it cannot be broken."[36]

Another benefit of this is the relationships that are built within the group. As the saying goes, "A family that prays together, stays together." Such is the case when brothers and sisters in Christ pray together too. A bond is forged and strengthened with each Rosary prayed.

I've had the pleasure of experiencing this first hand. When my oldest kids were very young, a few other moms and I started a small Rosary group. We started by meeting regularly in a room at their Catholic school. When the chapel was built there, we met in the chapel, praying for our families and the school itself.

---

[35] *Ibid #132*
[36] *bid #134*

We then formed a garden group over the summer with our spouses and kids, where we grew fresh produce for the local food bank. We incorporated the Rosary into those garden meetings as well and prayed with our spouses and kids. We didn't know it at the beginning, but the real blessing of that group was not just increased enrollment for the school or produce for the food bank. It was the relationships that were formed... between us moms, our spouses and our kids.

Even though we have since moved away from that town, even though we don't see each other on a regular basis, our bond remains, and I attribute this to the way we began—with the Rosary.

Rosary Prayer Group Chart for Five People

Write the names of each person assigned to each decade on the line provided. It is advisable to photo copy this and switch decades at least once a month so that you are meditating on other mysteries. If each person says one decade daily, your group will be saying an entire 5-decade Rosary daily.

Decade #1: _____

Opening Prayers as well as the First Mystery. Mondays and Saturdays: The Annunciation, Tuesdays and Fridays: the Agony in the Garden, Wednesdays and Sundays: The Resurrection, Thursdays: the Baptism of Jesus

Decade #2:_____

Mondays and Saturdays: The Visitation, Tuesdays and Fridays: the Scourging at the Pillar, Wednesdays and Sundays: The Ascension, Thursdays: the Wedding at Cana

Decade #3:_____

Mondays and Saturdays: The Nativity, Tuesdays and Fridays: the Crowning with Thorns, Wednesdays and Sundays: The Descent of the Holy Spirit, Thursdays: the Proclamation of the Kingdom

Decade #4_____

Mondays and Saturdays: The Presentation, Tuesdays and Fridays: the Carrying of the Cross, Wednesdays and Sundays: The Assumption, Thursdays: the Transfiguration

Decade #5:_____

The closing prayers as well as the Fifth Mystery. Mondays and Saturdays: The Finding in the Temple, Tuesdays and Fridays: the Crucifixion, Wednesdays and Sundays: The Coronation, Thursdays: the Institution of the Eucharist

CHAPTER ELEVEN:

How to Pray the Rosary: They Prayers, Mysteries & Meditations

By now, some of you newcomers may be convinced the Rosary is a powerful prayer—you may want to start praying the it—but maybe you are still intimidated by _how_ to pray it. Don't fret. It is my hope that those of you who have never prayed the Rosary before can turn to this chapter regularly, daily, and follow the prayers, step by step in this chapter. Below I have included the diagram again and step by step instructions with the words to the prayers. For the Rosary veterans who already know how to pray the Rosary, perhaps you can still benefit from the meditations I have written at the end of this chapter.

THE ROSARY STEP BY STEP

1. **State your intention for this Rosary or pray an opening prayer listed above.**
2. **On the cross, pray the Apostles Creed:** _I believe in God, the Father Almighty, Creator of heaven and earth; and in Jesus Christ, His only Son, our Lord: Who was conceived by the Holy Spirit, born of the Virgin Mary; suffered under Pontius Pilate, was crucified, died and was buried. He descended into hell; the third day He rose again from the dead; He ascended into heaven, is_

seated at the right hand of God the Father
Almighty; from thence He shall come to judge
the living and the dead. I believe in the Holy
Spirit, the Holy Catholic Church, the communion
of Saints, the forgiveness of sins, the
resurrection of the body, and life everlasting.
Amen.

3. **On the first bead, pray the Our Father:** *Our
Father, Who art in Heaven, hallowed be Thy
name; Thy Kingdom come, Thy will be done on
earth as it is in Heaven. Give us this day our
daily bread; and forgive us our trespasses as we
forgive those who trespass against us; and lead
us not into temptation, but deliver us from evil.
Amen.*

4. **On the next three consecutive beads pray the
Hail Mary for the virtues of faith, hope and
love:** *Hail Mary full of Grace, the Lord is with
thee. Blessed are thou among women and
blessed is the fruit of thy womb Jesus. Holy
Mary Mother of God, pray for us sinners now
and at the hour of our death Amen.*

5. **Now, consider the First Mystery (a listing of
the mysteries and meditations begin on page
124).**

6. **Pray one Our Father**

7. **Pray a Hail Mary on each of the next ten beads
while meditating on the First Mystery.**

8. **After ten Hail Mary's pray the Gloria:** *Glory be
to the Father, and to the Son, and to the Holy
Spirit. As it was in the beginning, is now and
every shall be. A world without end. Amen.*

9. **Pray the Fatima prayer dictated to the shepherd children:** *O my Jesus, forgive us our sins. Save us from the fires of Hell. Lead all souls into Heaven, especially those who are in most need of Thy Mercy.*

10. **Consider the Second Mystery**

11. **Pray one Our Father on the separated bead**

12. **Pray a Hail Mary on each of the next ten beads while meditating on the Second Mystery.**

13. **After ten Hail Mary's pray the Gloria**

14. **Pray the Fatima prayer dictated to the shepherd children**

15. **Consider the Third Mystery**

16. **Pray one Our Father on the separated bead**

17. **Pray a Hail Mary on each of the next ten beads while meditating on the Third Mystery.**

18. **After ten Hail Mary's pray the Gloria**

19. **Pray the Fatima prayer dictated to the shepherd children**

20. **Consider the Fourth Mystery**

21. **Pray one Our Father on the separated bead**

22. **Pray a Hail Mary on each of the next ten beads while meditating on the Fourth Mystery.**

23. **After ten Hail Mary's pray the Gloria**

24. **Pray the Fatima prayer dictated to the shepherd children**

25. **Consider the Fifth Mystery**

26. **Pray one Our Father on the separated bead**

27. **Pray a Hail Mary on each of the next ten beads while meditating on the Fifth Mystery.**

28. **After ten Hail Mary's pray the Gloria**

29. **Pray the Fatima prayer dictated to the shepherd children**

30. *Pray the Hail Holy Queen:* *Hail, holy Queen, Mother of mercy, hail, our life, our sweetness and our hope. To thee do we cry, poor banished children of Eve: to thee do we send up our sighs, mourning and weeping in this vale of tears. Turn then, most gracious Advocate, thine eyes of mercy toward us, and after this our exile, show unto us the blessed fruit of thy womb, Jesus, O merciful, O loving, O sweet Virgin Mary! Amen.*

31. **Pray the closing prayers of the Rosary:** *O God, whose only-begotten Son, by His life, death and resurrection, has purchased for us the rewards of eternal life; grant, we beseech Thee, that, meditating upon these mysteries of the Most Holy Rosary of the Blessed Virgin Mary, we may imitate what they contain and obtain what they promise, through the same Christ our Lord. Amen.*

32. **Pray One Our Father, One Hail Mary, and One Gloria for the Holy Father**

THE OPENING PRAYER

As you begin to pray your Rosary it is a good idea to start with an opening prayer. Below are a few variations to choose from.

The Confraternity Prayer: To be said by those who have enrolled in the Confraternity (Taken from Rosary-Center.org).

Queen of the Most Holy Rosary and Mother of us all, we come to you for help in our sorrows, trials and necessities. Sin leaves us weak and helpless but Divine Grace heals and strengthens. We ask for the grace to love Jesus as you loved Him, to believe as you believed, to hope as you hoped; we ask to share your purity of mind and heart. Give us true sorrow for sin and make us love people as you and Jesus loved them. Obtain for us the gifts of the Holy Spirit that we may be wise with your wisdom, understand with your understanding, know with your knowledge, prudent with your prudence, patient with your patience, courageous with your fortitude and desire justice ardently for everyone with the all consuming desire of the Sacred Heart of Jesus your Son. Open our minds that as we pray the Rosary we will understand the teachings of the Gospel contained in its mysteries.

We pray especially for the members of the Rosary Confraternity whom we love. Help them wherever they may be; guide them, watch over them and make them strong in their trials and suffering. We are drawn together by a common bond of great charity for you and for each other; keep us faithful to your Son and to your Rosary till death. Intercede for the souls in Purgatory, especially for the members of the Rosary Confraternity who have died. May they rest in peace. Finally, we ask for grace of final perseverance for ourselves and for our loved ones that we may all be reunited in heaven forever. Saint Dominic, you who received so much Grace and Strength from the Rosary, Pray for Us

A General Offering

I offer this Rosary for the intentions of the Blessed Virgin Mary, in reparation for the sins committed against Her Immaculate Heart and the Mournful Heart of Jesus, in reparation for my sins and those of the whole world. I also offer this Rosary for an end to abortion, for the protection of my marriage and children, and for peace on earth.

A Binding Prayer for Parents:

I bind to this Rosary my spouse and my children, all my family (immediate, extended, in-laws, living and deceased), my friends, my company, and my co-workers. I bind my children's friends, teachers, future spouses and their families. I bind to this Rosary all those who I said I would pray for. I bind all the priests who have ever distributed a Sacrament to me, prayed for me, or counseled me. I bind our President, his advisors, team, and family. I bind all leaders, lawmakers and military. I bind to this Rosary all those who will die today, and all the souls in Purgatory (especially the souls who suffer the most, and the ones who have no one to pray for them). I bind the Pope and all religious laity.

I ask for protection from distraction while I pray this Rosary, and the grace to enter the mysteries. I pray all this in Jesus' Name. Amen.

The Prayer Group Open:

I unite spiritually with all those in my Rosary prayer group. I offer these prayers in reparation for the sins of the world, for an end to abortion, for peace on earth, for the intentions of everyone in the group, and for my own personal intentions (State Intentions Here). May the grace and protection of Almighty God and His Mother be upon us, and all those we love. Amen.

THE MYSTERIES OF THE ROSARY

MONDAYS AND SATURDAYS

On Mondays and Saturdays, we meditate on the Joyful Mysteries of the Rosary: The Annunciation, the Visitation, the Nativity, The Presentation, and the Finding in the Temple. Below are a few different meditation variations to choose from.

Scriptural Mysteries for Mondays and Saturdays: Meditating on the Verses from the Bible

1. **The Annunciation:** "Then the angel said to her, "Do not be afraid, Mary, for you have found favor with God. Behold, you will conceive in your womb and bear a son, and you shall name him Jesus." (Luke 1:30-31)

2. **The Visitation:** "When Elizabeth heard Mary's greeting, the infant leaped in her womb, and Elizabeth, filled with the holy Spirit, cried out in a loud voice and said, "Most blessed are you among women, and blessed is the fruit of your womb." (Luke 1:41-42)

3. **The Nativity:** "For today in the city of David a savior has been born for you who is Messiah and Lord. And this will be a sign for you: you will find an infant wrapped in swaddling clothes and lying in a manger." (Luke 2:11-12)

4. **The Presentation:** "Simeon blessed them and said to Mary his mother, "Behold, this child is destined for the fall and rise of many in Israel, and to be a sign that will be contradicted (and you yourself a sword will pierce) so that the thoughts of many hearts may be revealed." (Luke 2:34-35)

5. **The Finding in the Temple:** "When his parents saw him, they were astonished, and his mother said to him, "Son, why have you done this to us? Your father and I have been looking for you with great anxiety. And he said to them, "Why were you looking for me? Did you not know that I must be in my Father's house?" (Luke 2:48-49)

Living Water Mysteries for Mondays and Saturdays: Praying for an Outpouring of the Holy Spirit

1. **The Annunciation:** Mary Refuge of Holy Love, protect my faith. Implore Your Spouse on my behalf that I may receive the grace to imitate Your faith at the Annunciation. Oh Most Holy Spirit, Living Water of God, nourish the seed within me, that I may grow in faith, believe Your messages in my heart, and surrender to the Father's Divine Will. Oh Holy Ghost, come, revitalize the faith of all the earth.

2. **The Visitation:** Mary Refuge of Holy Love, inspire me with your perfect charity. Implore your spouse on my behalf that I might receive the grace to imitate your servitude at the visitation. Oh, Mot Holy Spirit, Living Water of God, fill me to overflowing that I may pour out your fruits upon those the Father has placed in my life. Oh Holy Ghost, come, unite the hearts of all those on earth.

3. **The Nativity:** Mary Refuge of Holy Love, allow me to unite myself to your heart. Implore your spouse on my behalf that, like you, I too may receive the grace to behold, worthily, the fruit of your womb, made present in the Holy Eucharist. Oh Most Holy Spirit, Living Water of God, wash me of any pride found in my heart. Make me as humble a dwelling as the stable in which Jesus was first born. Oh Holy Ghost, come, prepare the hearts of all the earth.

4. **The Presentation:** Mary Refuge of Holy Love, teach me how to die to myself. Implore your spouse on my behalf that I may receive the grace to imitate the holy submission you

displayed at the Presentation. Oh Most Holy Spirit, Living Water of God, swallow me up in your current so that I can allow myself to be led down the stream of salvation by your power and by the wisdom of the superiors God has placed in my life. Oh Holy Ghost, come, engulf the hearts of all the earth.

5. **The Finding in the Temple:** Mary Refuge of Holy Love, guide me on my search for your son. Implore your spouse on my behalf that I may receive the grace to know deeply the joy of the finding in the temple. Oh Most Holy Spirit, Living Water of God, I know you flow in the direction of Jesus, lead me to him, that I too may sit at his feet and hear Him preach of the Father. Oh Holy Ghost, come, carry home all the hearts of all the earth.

Healing Mysteries for Mondays and Saturdays: Praying for Physical Healing of Sickness or Disease

1. **The Annunciation:** Immaculate Heart of Mary: You found favor with God. And at the moment of Your consent to the Divine Will, the Sacred Heart of Jesus was formed in You. He was forever joined to Your Heart. Through You, He came and brought life and healing—in all manner of disease and all manner of sickness. Compassionate Mother, we come to You seeking Your intercession, as we have not found such favor with God. But Mother, we have such

need of healing. Please bring forth into our midst Thy Son, our Divine Physician. Plead to Him on our behalf, that He may heal (State Name) of his/her illness. Oh, United Hearts of Jesus and Mary: I beg You. Take (Name's) heart into Your Hearts and restore his/her health!

2. **The Visitation:** Immaculate Heart of Mary: when You visited St. Elizabeth, she believed that You carried the Savior; she was instantly filled with the Holy Spirit. And the life within her leaped in her womb at the Presence of Your United Hearts. Blessed Mother, we too, believe....not only that You carried Him in Your womb, but that You are even now united to His Sacred Heart. We trust in Jesus' words to the faithful centurion, "as thou hast believed, so be it done unto thee." We believe that, just as Jesus healed the servant, He can heal (Name). Mother of Mercy, come to (Name's) aid as You did Elizabeth's, that she/he may also be filled with the Holy Spirit and the life within him/her touched by the power of God. Oh, United Hearts of Jesus and Mary: I beg You. Take (Name's) heart into Your Hearts and restore his/her health!

3. **The Nativity:** Immaculate Heart of Mary: As You touched Your Baby, Jesus, to Your Heart, the shepherds approached You. They placed gifts before You and Your Son. They worshipped Him ardently, with faith that He was in fact the Savior of souls. Blessed Mother, I now approach You. I place this humble prayer for (Name)

129

before You and Your Son. Touch it to Your Heart, united to the Sacred Heart of Jesus. Plead to Him on (Name's) behalf as we ardently worship Him...with faith that, just as Jesus healed Peter's mother-in-law by touching her hand, so too can He heal (Name) by touching him/her. Oh, United Hearts of Jesus and Mary: I beg You. Take (Name's) heart into Your Hearts and restore his/her health!

4. **The Presentation**: Immaculate Heart of Mary: Humbly, You took Your Son to the Temple and presented Him to God. There You received prophesy that a sword shall pierce Your Heart also. Despite the anguish it caused You, You kept this to yourself, and suffered it faithfully and courageously for souls. Blessed Mother, (Name's) heart has been pierced in a special way—with (state illness). Yet she/he has suffered courageously and faithfully, despite the anguish it no doubt causes her/him. Please, have compassion on her/him. Go to Your Son on her/his behalf and present to our God these humble prayers for healing. We believe it is true, that "He laid His hands on every one of them, and healed them." Beg for this grace for (Name) that through her/his healing, the Father may be glorified through the Son. Oh, United Hearts of Jesus and Mary: I beg You. Take (Name's) heart into Your Hearts and restore his/her health!

5. **The Finding in the Temple**: Immaculate Heart of Mary: You searched long and hard, and with an

aching Heart, for Your Son. He was found preaching fervently in the Temple, mystifying the doctors and scholars and bringing glory to the Father. Yet, when He saw You, He accompanied You back to the caravan as You wished. Blessed Mother, (Name) has searched long and hard, and with an aching Heart, for a cure. Please Mother, go to Thy Son on his/her behalf, that He may accompany You to (Name). We need Him, Mother. We believe He "cast out the spirits with a word, and healed all that were sick." May Jesus now heal (Name) and thereby mystify the doctors and scholars and bring glory to the Father. Oh, United Hearts of Jesus and Mary: I beg You. Take (Name's) heart into Your Hearts and restore his/her health!

The Mysteries of Grace for Mondays and Saturdays: Praying for the Grace of the Joyful Mysteries

1. **The Annunciation**: While She was in prayer, the angel Gabriel appeared to Mary, revealing God's Will for her life—to have a baby, which was by no means easy. Mary, though, courageously said yes to God's plan. With Her yes, the Holy Spirit came upon Her and Jesus dwelled within Her. Mary, while I am in prayer here now, grant me the grace to hear the will of God for my life. And grant me the grace to consent to it, to give my resounding yes! May

131

this enable the Lord Jesus to dwell within me and the Holy Spirit to come upon me.

2. **The Visitation:** The Virgin Mary visited Elizabeth who was pregnant and in need. Upon Her arrival Elizabeth recognized, through the Holy Spirit, the presence of the Son of God within Her. Elizabeth spoke out in praise, and the life within Her leaped. Mary, I too, am in need right now. Grant me the grace of experiencing your Holy visit. Through the Holy Spirit, may I too recognize the presence of the Son of God who is with You eternally, and now, through these prayers, in my midst.

3. **The Nativity:** While in Bethlehem, Joseph and Mary were rejected. There was no room at the Inn and the time had come for Jesus to be delivered. So, they accepted a small stable as their cover, and laid the Baby Jesus in a manger. Mary, grant me the grace to accept situations, even though they are not my first desire. Help me to see that God's plan is in humility and simplicity... that His ways are so far above my ways. Through your grace do not allow me to reject You and Your Son, as the innkeepers did at Bethlehem.

4. **The Presentation:** Mary and Joseph obediently took Baby Jesus to the Temple to be blessed, where they met Simeon, who gave thanks to God for being allowed to see and hold the Messiah. He also prophesied of the coming heartache that Mary would have to experience. And She held this revelation in Her Heart. Mary,

grant me the grace of obedience, that I may do what God has called me to through the laws of His Church. Help me to see and behold the Messiah, and to hold the revelation of His Word in my heart.

5. **The Finding of Jesus in the Temple:** Mary and Joseph set out towards home, from Jerusalem, with a caravan of family and friends. Mary and Joseph assumed Jesus was among them in the caravan. But after quite some time, they discovered He was not. They traveled a great distance, back to Jerusalem, where they found Him teaching and preaching in the Temple. Mary, grant me the grace to conduct a fruitful examination of conscience. Do not allow me to merely assume Jesus is with me. Help me to take inventory of my heart, so that I do not travel any distance from Him.

TUESDAYS AND FRIDAYS

On Tuesdays and Fridays, we meditate on the Sorrowful Mysteries of the Rosary: the Agony in the Garden, the Scourging at the Pillar, the Crowning with Thorns, the Carrying of the Cross, and the Crucifixion. Below are a few different meditation variations to choose from.

Scriptural Mysteries for Tuesdays and Fridays: Meditating on the Verses from the Bible

1. **The Agony in the Garden:** "Then he said to them, "My soul is sorrowful even to death. Remain here and keep watch with me. He advanced a little and fell prostrate in prayer, saying, "My Father, if it is possible, let this cup pass from me; yet, not as I will, but as you will." (Mt. 26:38-39)

2. **The Scourging at the Pillar:** "Yet it was our pain that he bore, our sufferings he endured. We thought of him as stricken, struck down by God and afflicted, But he was pierced for our sins, crushed for our iniquity. He bore the punishment that makes us whole, by his wounds we were healed." (Is. 53:4-5)

3. **The Crowning with Thorns:** "And the soldiers wove a crown out of thorns and placed it on his head, and clothed him in a purple cloak, and they came to him and said, "Hail, King of the Jews!" And they struck him repeatedly." (John 19:2-3)

4. **The Carrying of the Cross:** "As they led him away they took hold of a certain Simon, a Cyrenian, who was coming in from the country; and after laying the cross on him, they made him carry it behind Jesus. A large crowd of people followed Jesus, including many women who mourned and lamented him." (Luke 23:26-27)

5. **The Crucifixion:** "Jesus cried out in a loud voice, "Father, into your hands I commend my spirit"; and when he had said this he breathed his last. The centurion who witnessed what had

happened glorified God and said, "This man was innocent* beyond doubt." (Luke 23: 46-47)

Living Water Mysteries for Tuesdays and Fridays: Praying for an Outpouring of the Holy Spirit

1. **The Agony in the Garden:** Mary Refuge of Holy Love, comfort your child. Implore your spouse on my behalf that I may receive the grace to imitate the surrender Jesus displayed in the Agony in the Garden. Oh Most Holy Spirit, Living Water of God, wash away all anxiety in my heart, that I may trust in the Divine Will of God and resolve to drink of the cup prepared for me. Help me to calmly accept all things as from the hand of the Father. Oh Holy Ghost, come, bring peace to the hearts of all the earth.

2. **The Scourging at the Pillar:** Mary Refuge of Holy Love, sustain me with your grace. Implore your spouse on my behalf that I may receive the grace of endurance which Jesus displayed for love of us at the Scourging at the Pillar. Oh Most Holy Spirit, Living Water of God, saturate my being that I may undertake a life of physical denial and suffer any pain the Father wills to send me in reparation for my sins and those of the whole world. Oh Holy Ghost, come, strengthen the hearts of all the earth.

3. **The Crowning with Thorns:** Mary Refuge of Holy Love, lend me your profound humility. Implore your spouse on my behalf that I may

receive the grace to imitate the submission Jesus displayed at the Crowning with Thorns. Oh Most Holy Spirit, Living Water of God, fill me to overflowing that I too may suffer humiliations and persecutions with patience and love in order to be a living example of our merciful, loving savior. Oh Holy Ghost, come, humble the hearts of all the earth.

4. **The Carrying of the Cross:** Mary Refuge of Holy Love, pray for me in my time of need. Implore your spouse on my behalf that I may receive the grace of perseverance which Jesus displayed in His carrying of the Cross. Oh Most Holy Spirit, Living Water of God, nourish my body and soul that I may find the strength to continue in the Christian life, especially at those points where I must carry my own cross. Oh Holy Ghost, come, revive the souls of all the earth.

5. **The Crucifixion**: Mary Refuge of Holy Love, be near me now and at the hour of my death. Implore your spouse on my behalf that I may receive the grace to see the glorious Divine Will hidden beneath the tragedy of the Crucifixion. Oh Most Holy Spirit, Living Water of God, still the ripples of my mind and calm my fears that I may see, not with the eyes of flesh but the crystal clear waters of your infinite wisdom. Oh Holy Ghost, come, bring understanding to the hearts of all the earth.

Healing Mysteries for Tuesdays and Fridays: Praying for Physical Healing of Sickness or Disease

1. **Agony in the Garden:** Immaculate Heart of Mary: Your Son suffered such Agony in the Garden as He saw what He would have to undergo to make all things anew. Even still, He had such unfathomable love and compassion for souls that He agreed to the Father's Will in spite of all that awaited Him. Blessed Mother, for the sake of all that He suffered in the garden that night; plead to Jesus on behalf of (Name)— for all that he/she now suffers. Petition the Sacred Heart of Jesus, Who can refuse You nothing, to pour out His love and compassion on (Name), to make him/her anew and heal him/her. We believe the Word which says, "she touched Him, and...she was healed immediately." Oh, United Hearts of Jesus and Mary: I beg You. Take (Name's) heart into Your Hearts and restore his/her health!

2. **The Scourging at the Pillar:** Immaculate Heart of Mary: Who can imagine what You felt as You watched what became of Your Son's most Sacred Body. Who can know the physical pain He underwent in order that souls might be cleansed by His Blood. Blessed Mother, for the sake of all He endured at the Scourging, plead to Jesus on behalf of (Name)—for all the that she now endures with his/her illness. Petition the Sacred Heart of Jesus, Who can refuse You nothing, to cleanse him/her of all iniquity and

disease. We place our trust in the Word which says, "and them that had need of healing He cured." Oh, United Hearts of Jesus and Mary: I beg You. Take (Name's) heart into Your Hearts and restore his/her health!

3.   **The Crowning with Thorns**: Immaculate Heart of Mary: Your Son, our eternal King, humbled Himself to such mockery! Yet You remained confident in His Divine power and the Father's Divine Will. Blessed Mother for the sake of all that He accepted at the Crowning, plead to Jesus on (Name's) behalf, for all that he/she accepts through this (illness). Oh Mary, our Queen, we now humble ourselves before You. We are confident in the power of Jesus; we believe the Word which says, "for power came forth from Him, and healed [them] all." Oh gracious Advocate, petition the Sacred Heart of Jesus, Who can refuse You nothing, that He might heal (Name) of all sickness and malady. Oh, United Hearts of Jesus and Mary: I beg You. Take (Name's) heart into Your Hearts and restore his/her health!

4.   **Jesus Carries the Cross:** Immaculate Heart of Mary: Your Son embraced the Cross; He carried it with such love for souls, that all might be reconciled to the Father. Blessed Mother, for the sake of His perseverance in Carrying the Cross, plead to Jesus on (Name's) behalf for the way that she too, has persevered in carrying his/her cross. Oh Gracious Advocate, petition the Sacred Heart of Jesus, Who can refuse You

nothing, that He might have compassion on (Name)and heal him/ her. We trust that Scripture is true, "He had compassion on them, and healed their sick." And we pray that his/her healing will glorify God and reconcile all to the Father. Oh, United Hearts of Jesus and Mary: I beg You. Take (Name's) heart into Your Hearts and restore her health!

5. **The Crucifixion:** Immaculate Heart of Mary: The death of Your Son brought life to all the world. The Blood He shed not only opened the grave and opened Heaven for all, but it opened the human heart as well. Blessed Mother, for the sake of the suffering of the Crucified Christ, plead to Your Son on (Name's) behalf for all that he/she now suffers. Oh Gracious Advocate, petition the Sacred Heart of Jesus, Who can refuse You nothing, that He will remove the illness within him/ her. We fall at Your feet with faith in the Word, "they cast them down at this feet; and he healed them." Oh, United Hearts of Jesus and Mary: I beg You. Take (Name's) heart into Your Hearts and restore his/her health!

The Mysteries of Grace for Tuesdays and Fridays: Praying for the Grace of the Sorrowful Mysteries

1. **The Agony in the Garden:** The night before His Passion, Jesus went to the Garden of Gethsemane to pray. His closest friends fell asleep and He was alone. He foresaw all that He

would suffer, and all the souls that would be lost in spite His sufferings. This caused Him such agony and distress that He sweat blood. But He consented to the Father's Will and accepted His Passion. Mary, in all the anxieties of my life, grant me the grace to accept the Father's Will. Help me to stay awake to the fact that the sufferings of my life are nothing compared to what your Son experienced. May the time I spend with Him, during this decade, comfort Him for all that He still suffers on account of indifferent souls, asleep in faith.

2. **The Scourging at the Pillar:** The soldiers tied Jesus to a pole, stripped off His garments, and began to beat Him cruelly. Their instruments gouged Jesus' sacred flesh to such a degree that His bone was exposed. Every inch of Him was wounded beyond recognition, but He offered this torture for our sake. Mary, grant me the grace to endure the pains of my physical body. Remind me that they are nothing compared to what Your Son endured. Give me the inspiration and the heart to offer these afflictions to God on behalf of sinners. May the time I spend with Him, during this decade, comfort Him for all that He still suffers on account of those who mistreat His Body and Blood in the Eucharist.

3. **The Crowning with Thorns:** After His flogging, Jesus was dressed for mockery in a purple cloak. The soldiers placed a crown of large, sharp thorns on His Head. They pressed it into His skull and proceeded to mock, hit, and spit at

Him. All the while, Jesus remained silent. Even though they were wrong—even though Jesus really is a King—they were not able to see Him or understand the truth of who He is. So He opened not His mouth. Mary, grant me the grace to always see Him and to always understand His truth. Never let me hurt Him with cynicism or doubt. Petition Him to not be silent. I am open and listening. May the time I spend with Him, during this decade, comfort Him for all He still suffers on account of those who openly mock the Catholic Church and its people.

4. **The Carrying of the Cross:** The soldiers gave Jesus His Cross and led Him to Golgatha. The women who followed Him wept bitterly. Jesus was so weak from His torture that He fell multiple times under the weight of the cross. Finally, they forced a man named Simon of Cyrene to help Jesus carry it the rest of the way. Mary, grant me the grace of perseverance, so that with every step today, I will willingly shoulder my crosses. In my weak moments, where I am falling under the weight of them, come to my aid, Mother. Help me as Simon helped Your Son. May the time I spend with Him, during this decade, comfort Him for all He still suffers on account of those who reject their crosses and refuse to help their neighbor.

5. **The Crucifixion:** In His last moments on the cross, Jesus gave His holy Mother to the apostle, John, which symbolized Him giving Her

to all of us. He prayed that the Heavenly Father forgive his executioners. Then, He gave up His spirit. Mary, grant me the grace to receive You as my Mother, with new charity and appreciation. Grant me the grace to forgive those who do me wrong. And give me the grace to surrender my spirit into the Hands of God. May the time I spend with Him, during this decade, comfort Him for all that He still suffers on account of those who refuse You as their Mother, as well as those who are perishing in unforgiveness.

WEDNESDAYS AND SUNDAYS

On Wednesdays and Sundays, we meditate on the Glorious Mysteries of the Rosary: The Resurrection, the Ascension, the Descent of the Holy Spirit, the Assumption, and the Coronation. Below are a few different meditation variations to choose from.

Scriptural Mysteries for Wednesdays and Sundays: Meditating on the Verses from the Bible

1. **The Resurrection:** On entering the tomb they saw a young man sitting on the right side, clothed in a white robe, and they were utterly amazed. He said to them, "Do not be amazed! You seek Jesus of Nazareth, the crucified. He has been raised; he is not here. Behold, the place where they laid him." (Mark 16:5-6)

2. **The Ascension:** While they were looking intently at the sky as he was going, suddenly two men dressed in white garments stood beside them. They said, "Men of Galilee, why are you standing there looking at the sky? This Jesus who has been taken up from you into heaven will return in the same way as you have seen him going into heaven." (Acts 1:10-11)

3. **The Descent of the Holy Spirit:** "And suddenly there came from the sky a noise like a strong driving wind, and it filled the entire house in which they were. Then there appeared to them tongues as of fire, which parted and came to rest on each one of them. And they were all filled with the holy Spirit and began to speak in different tongues, as the Spirit enabled them to proclaim." (Acts 2:2-4)

4. **The Assumption:** "Then God's temple in heaven was opened, and the ark of his covenant could be seen in the temple. There were flashes of lightning, rumblings, and peals of thunder, an earthquake, and a violent hailstorm... A great sign appeared in the sky, a woman* clothed with the sun, with the moon under her feet, and on her head a crown of twelve stars." (Rev. 11:19 and 12:1)

5. **The Coronation:** "From now on the crown of righteousness awaits me, which the Lord, the just judge, will award to me on that day, and not only to me, but to all who have longed for his appearance." (2 Timothy 4:8)

Living Water Mysteries for Wednesdays and Sundays: Praying for an Outpouring of the Holy Spirit

1. **The Resurrection:** Mary Refuge of Holy Love, purify me. Implore your spouse on my behalf that I may receive the grace to be made worthy of the promise of the resurrection. Oh Most Holy Spirit, Living Water of God, flood my dry spirit. Revive my dry soul. Unite me with my redeemer so that with him, I might rise above temptation, apathy, sin and even death itself. Oh Holy Ghost, come, renew the face of the earth.

2. **The Ascension:** Mary Refuge of Holy Love, shine your light on me. Implore your spouse on my behalf that I may receive the grace of hope as seen in the Ascension of our Lord. Oh Most Holy Spirit, Living Water of God, consume me. Wrap me in your Breath as in clouds and lift me to the heights of Heaven, to the heights of salvation and union with the Lord. Oh Holy Ghost, come, sanctify hearts on earth.

3. **The Decent of the Holy Spirit:** Mary Refuge of Holy Love, shed your grace on me. Implore your spouse on my behalf that I may receive the grace of fervor that comes from the Descent of the Holy Spirit. Oh Most Holy Spirit, Living Water of God, fill me. Give me your gifts that I may go out with boldness and give witness to faith. Oh Holy Ghost, come, revive the Church of Jesus Christ on Earth.

4. **The Assumption:** Mary Refuge of Holy Love, shed your grace on me. Implore your spouse on my behalf that I may receive the grace of hope that is seen in the mystery of the Assumption. Oh Most Holy Spirit, Living Water of God, purify me. Make me more like your Spouse, the holy and Blessed Virgin Mary, that I may be found pure and without sin on my last day. Oh Holy Ghost, come, cleanse the hearts of your people.

5. **The Coronation:** Mary Refuge of Holy Love, shed your grace on me. Implore your spouse on my behalf that I may receive the grace of triumph that is seen in the mystery of the Coronation. Oh Most Holy Spirit, Living Water of God, crown me with your glory. Make me a worthy heir to the King and Queen of Heaven, that I may enjoy paradise with them for all eternity. Oh Holy Ghost, come, instate us as beneficiaries of the Almighty.

Healing Mysteries for Wednesdays and Sundays: Praying for Physical Healing of Sickness or Disease

1. **The Resurrection:** Immaculate Heart of Mary: Your Son, our Savior, the Lord Jesus Christ, rose to new life and with Him arose many others as well. He healed them of death itself and they walked into the city, giving witness of Him and glory to God. Oh Holy Mary, plead to Your Son, Who can refuse You nothing, on behalf of (Name). May He by the power of His

145

Resurrection heal him/her; may he/she rise above this illness and everywhere he/she goes give witness to Him and glory to God. May it be done according to the Word, "When he saw that he was healed, turned back, with a loud voice glorifying God." Oh, United Hearts of Jesus and Mary: I beg You. Take (Name's) heart into Your Hearts and restore his/her health!

2. **The Ascension:** Immaculate Heart of Mary: You watched as Your Son ascended out of sight. But He did not leave You abandoned. In fact, He left with the promise of remaining with all of us under the form of bread and wine in the Holy Eucharist. Oh Holy Mary, plead to Your Son, Who can refuse You nothing, on behalf of (Name). May the power of His Real Presence, now residing within him/her, touch his/her heart. May He reach out from the Holy Eucharist inside him/her and heal him/her. We trust in Him, Who in Scriptures, "laid His hands on every one of them, and healed them." Oh, United Hearts of Jesus and Mary: I beg You. Take (Name's) heart into Your Hearts and restore her health!

3. **The Descent of the Holy Spirit:** Immaculate Heart of Mary: Your Spouse descended upon You and the apostles that first Pentecost, relieving fears, strengthening hearts, and healing them of their inability to preach the Good News. Oh Holy Mary, plead to Your Son, Who can refuse You nothing, on behalf of (Name). May He send the power of the Holy

Spirit into his/her heart. May He relieve his/her fears, strengthen him/her and heal him/her...to such a capacity that he/she resounds of the Good News. We trust in Scripture, which says, "Them that had need of healing he cured." Oh, United Hearts of Jesus and Mary: I beg You. Take (Name's) heart into Your Hearts and restore his/her health!

4. **The Assumption:** Immaculate Heart of Mary: You were sinless unto death and Your Son could not allow Your most pure Body to suffer the effects of the grave...so He assumed You into Heaven to be forever united with Himself. What a gift for You—and for us all, as You now come through time and space to be with us, to aid us, protect us and intercede for us. Oh Holy Mary, plead to Your Son, Who can refuse You nothing, on behalf of (Name). May the power of Your United Hearts envelop hhim/er and heal him/her. We trust in the Divine Physician Who said, "I say unto thee, Arise, and take up thy couch..." And immediately the man rose up... and was healed. Oh, United Hearts of Jesus and Mary: I beg You. Take (Name's) heart into Your Hearts and restore her health!

5. **The Coronation:** Immaculate Heart of Mary: Upon Your glorious arrival into Heaven You were crowned Queen of all Heaven and all earth. You are the delight of the angels and saints, the hope of those in Purgatory, and the sweet Refuge, Protectress, and Advocate for us pilgrims on earth. Oh Holy Queen, we beseech

Thee as Your children: plead to Your Son, Who can refuse You nothing, on behalf of (Name). At Your request may He unleash His power upon her. May He touch him/her heart. For we believe He can heal him/her, just as Scripture says He touched the soldier's ear, and healed him. Oh, United Hearts of Jesus and Mary: I beg You. Take (Name's) heart into Your Hearts and restore his/her health!

The Mysteries of Grace for Wednesdays and Sundays: Praying for the Grace of the Glorious Mysteries

1. **The Resurrection:** The women went to the tomb at dawn. They set out while it was still dark. This shows that He rose in darkness. He appeared to a converted sinner who He delivered of demons. Mary, grant me the grace to endure the dark night of this life. May Jesus deliver me from evil, forgive me of my sins, and let me see Him in the Resurrection.

2. **The Ascension**: The disciples who witnessed His resurrection, walked with Him. And at the appointed time were commissioned into His ministry. They were called to continue His work, to go make disciples of all the earth. Mary grant me the grace to walk closely with Jesus. May be call and commission me to the work of evangelization, until He comes again on the clouds as He ascended.

3. **The Descent of the Holy Spirit:** After Jesus ascended, the apostles gathered with the Virgin Mary, fearful they too might suffer persecution or death. The Holy Spirit descended upon them equipping them with power to do the work Jesus called them to. Mary, grant me the grace to receive the fullness of the Holy Spirit during this Rosary. May the Lord five me the gifts I need to speak to people about our faith. And may He renew the face of the earth.

4. **The Assumption:** At the end of Her earthly life, the Virgin Mary was assumed into Heaven. Jesus did not allow Her sinless body—His first tabernacle—to suffer the decomposition of the grave. Rather, they were reunited in Heavenly glory. Mary, grant me the grace at the end of my earthly life to be united with Jesus. May He grant me mercy and pardon on the day so that my soul may be assumed in Heavenly glory. Oh, Jesus and Mary, make of me a great saint.

5. **The Coronation:** When Mary arrives in the Kingdom of Heaven She is crowned Queen of Heaven and Earth. She is the Mother of the King of Kings, the prince of Peace. She is the Daughter of the Almighty, and the Spouse of the Spirit. And so She is given a title worthy of this dignity. Mary, grant me the grace to be made worthy of the crown. May Jesus prepare a place for me and all my family and friends in the never-ending Kingdom of God.

THURSDAYS

On Thursdays, we meditate on the Luminous Mysteries of the Rosary: the Baptism of Jesus, the Wedding at Cana, the Proclamation of the Kingdom, the Transfiguration, and the Institution of the Eucharist. Below are a few different meditation variations to choose from.

Scriptural Mysteries for Thursdays: Meditating on the Verses from the Bible

1. **The Baptism of Jesus:** "After Jesus was baptized, he came up from the water and behold, the heavens were opened [for him], and he saw the Spirit of God descending like a dove [and] coming upon him. And a voice came from the heavens, saying, "This is my beloved Son, with whom I am well pleased." (Mt. 3:16-17)

2. **The Wedding at Cana:** "When the wine ran short, the mother of Jesus said to him, "They have no wine." [And] Jesus said to her, "Woman, how does your concern affect me? My hour has not yet come." His mother said to the servers, "Do whatever he tells you." (John 2:3-5)

3. **The Proclamation of the Kingdom:** After John had been arrested, Jesus came to Galilee proclaiming the gospel of God: "This is the time

of fulfillment. The kingdom of God is at hand. Repent, and believe in the gospel." (Mark 1:14-15)

4. **The Transfiguration:** "After six days Jesus took Peter, James, and John his brother, and led them up a high mountain by themselves. And he was transfigured before them; his face shone like the sun and his clothes became white as light. And behold, Moses and Elijah appeared to them, conversing with him." (Mt. 17:1-3)

5. **The Institution of the Eucharist:** Then he took the bread, said the blessing, broke it, and gave it to them, saying, "This is my body, which will be given for you; do this in memory of me." And likewise the cup after they had eaten, saying, "This cup is the new covenant in my blood, which will be shed for you. (Luke 22:19-20)

Living Water Mysteries for Thursdays: Praying for an Outpouring of the Holy Spirit

1. **The Baptism of Jesus:** Mary Refuge of Holy Love, keep me steadfast in my baptismal vows. Implore your spouse on my behalf that I may receive the grace of purity show to us at the baptism of Jesus. Oh Most Holy Spirit, Living Water of God, saturate my being. Keep me afloat in my journey. Wash me clean from my stain that I may ever imitate the Savior and that I too may be thus pleasing to the Father and

151

hear the sound of His voice in my heart. Oh Holy Ghost, come, rain down upon all the earth.

2. **The Wedding at Cana:** Mary Refuge of Holy Love, cast your compassionate glance toward me. Implore your spouse on my behalf that I too may experience the grace of transformation at the wedding at Cana. Oh Most Holy Spirit, Living Water of God, fill this empty vessel of my body and make me into a proper dwelling for the Lord Jesus. I so desire to be a witness to Our Lady's intercession, and Jesus' love and mercy and to thereby glorify the thrice-holy God. Oh Holy Ghost, come, transform the hearts of all the earth.

3. **The Proclamation of the Kingdom of God:** Mary Refuge of Holy Love, purify my heart of all worldly concern. Implore your spouse on my behalf that I may receive the grace to understand the hope of the Proclamation of the Kingdom of God. Oh Most Holy Spirit, Living Water of God, drown all temptations within me and pour fortitude into my soul that Thy Kingdom may come and settle into my heart. Oh Holy Ghost, come, free all the imprisoned souls on earth

4. **The Transfiguration:** Mary Refuge of Holy Love, lift the veil that hinders my vision. Implore your spouse on my behalf that I may receive the grace to see, like the apostles, the grandeur of the Transfiguration. Oh Most Holy Spirit, Living Water of God, rinse my eyes in your truth. Make clear the murky waters of compromise

and heresy so that none shall ever turn away from the glorified Jesus, who waits to transfigure us into Himself. Oh Holy Ghost, come, restore sight to the spiritually blind here on earth.

5. **The Institution of the Holy Eucharist:** Mary Refuge of Holy Love, teach me your immaculate ways. Implore your spouse on my behalf that I may receive the grace to worthily partake of the gift of the Holy Eucharist. Oh Most Holy Spirit, Living Water of God, saturate the soil of my soul with virtue and righteousness so that with each communion, Jesus, fruit of Mary's womb will find my heart to be an adequate garden in which to take root. Oh Holy Ghost, come, prepare the hearts of all the earth.

The Mysteries of Grace for Thursdays: Praying for the Grace of the Luminous Mysteries

The Baptism of Jesus: Jesus asks John the Baptist to baptize Him in the Jordan River. When He comes up from the water the Heavens are opened, and we hear that the Father is well-pleased. Mary, grant me the grace to follow Jesus and live up to my Baptismal vows. May the Heavenly Father be pleased with my efforts and on my last day, may the Heavens be opened up to me.

The Wedding at Cana: Through Mary's intercession, Jesus works His first miracle by changing regular water into strong wine. This opens the hearts of the disciples to believe in Him, to see Him as more than just a teacher. Mary, grant me the grace of faith, and the grace to believe more in Jesus' power and love. May He open my heart wider, and change me from a regular believer to a strong believer.

The Proclamation of the Kingdom: After the Heavens are opened and the hearts of believers are opened, Jesus proclaims the Kingdom of God is at hand. All the baptized must do to receive it, is repent and believe. Mary, grant me the grace of repentance and true sorrow for sin. Through the Sacrament of Reconciliation, may the Blood of Jesus restore me to citizenship in the Kingdom of God.

The Transfiguration: Jesus takes Peter, James, and John up Mr. Tabor and is transfigured into light. He is seen in resplendent glory. Moses and Elijah appear with Him (representing the law and the prophets). The Heavenly Father, speaks from on high and says, "Listen to Him." Mary, grant me the grace of total transformation. Through repentance and adherence to the law, and belief in the fulfillment of the prophets, may I too be transfigured in Christ Jesus, Your Son.

The Institution of the Eucharist: At the last supper, the night before He was to suffer and die, Jesus breaks bread with his apostles. He gives them the Sacrament of His Body and Blood, so that He can remain forever with us and in us. Mary, grant me the grace to worthily receive the holy Eucharist. Do not let me be a Judas—a betrayer at table with Your Son. Grant me a keen awareness of my sins, that I may repent of them all, prior to receiving Him.

Made in the USA
Middletown, DE
11 October 2023